Ethics & Professional Practice
for Neopagan Clergy

Also by Katherine MacDowell

Neopagan Theology Series

Sacred Groves: Creating & Sustaining Neopagan Covens
The Goddess Wheel of the Year
Ritual & Liturgy for Wiccan Clergy

Additional Works
Witness: A Collection of Poetry

Ethics & Professional Practice *for* Neopagan Clergy

Katherine MacDowell
D.DIV., D.TH., MA, M.ED., SH., HP., OCP

Ocean Seminary College
Lulu Press

ETHICS & PROFESSIONAL PRACTICE FOR NEOPAGAN CLERGY. Copyright © 2009 by Katherine MacDowell. All rights reserved. Unauthorized distribution, storing, or duplication either in print or online is strictly prohibited without author's written permission.

For further information, please write to:
Ocean Seminary College Press
OSCPress@OceanSeminaryCollege.org

Published by Lulu
North Carolina, USA
www.Lulu.com

First Edition

ISBN: 978-0-557-09718-0

Dedicated to Tom, who reminds me:
Sometimes there are no gray areas,
but right and wrong,
and it takes courage to do what is right.

Contents

One
Defining Ethics—An Introduction
1

Two
Theological Ethics of Neopaganism Defined
9

Three
Character & Worldview of the Priest/ess
23

Four
The Professional Role
35

Five
The Pastoral Relationship
47

Six
Power & Confidentiality
81

Seven
Sex & Multiple Relationships
93

Eight
Ethical Issues & Money
101

Nine
Working with Children & Adolescents
107

Ten
When to Refer
117

Eleven
Resolving Ethical Dilemmas
135

Twelve
Establishing an Ethical Code
171

Notes
About the Author

1
Defining Ethics— An Introduction

Ethics is a branch of philosophy that is concerned with defining right and wrong (and negotiating the gray areas between); as such it is traditionally referred to as *moral philosophy*. Further ethics refers to the systematic reflection upon moral definitions. Historically, the field of ethics emerged with theories of virtue in classical Greece, whereby virtue and human excellence were simultaneously defined in the word *arête*[1]. In Ancient Greece, the definitions of virtue were culturally constrained, illustrating the values of the time, such as courage, justice and moderation. As philosophy developed, these moral virtues were seen as necessary actions to bring about happiness. In this fashion, the ancient philosophers saw true happiness as an internally generated state that emerged based on how we conducted ourselves in the world around us. Since the time of Homer, the field of ethics has expanded.

In particular, and most relevant for a contemporary understanding of ethics as it impacts Neopagan theological framework, is the development of three central lines of inquiry: **metaethics, normative ethics**, and **applied ethics**. These three theoretical positions intersect when we begin to explore ethics and the parameters of professional practice within a religious leadership role in a Neopagan tradition. As such, this opening chapter will provide you with a basic introduction and understanding of these three areas of ethics, which in the next chapter will be further framed from a Neopagan perspective.

Metaethics

Metaethics refers to exploring morality from the position of ultimate origin or cause. In this fashion, metaethics looks at the over-arching cause for who or what defines right and wrong and questions pertaining to the primal origin of moral principles emerge from. In short, it is all about our attributing the emergence of personal moral principles or the moral principles within a wider cultural setting (such as religion, business, medicine, etc.) to some essential origin. These attributions in turn serve to justify or identify the authority of these principles. There are a multitude of ways individuals attribute the emergence of moral principles, which are the concern and focus of metaethics:

> **Divinely inspired or given** (either directly to a people or innately visible within individuals); as many of you reading this will know one of the most widely disseminated moral codes attributed to a divine author are the Mosaic Laws. We have seen how these laws, particularly within the Ten Commandments (which are actually only a small portion of the full laws), have influenced the legal and social structures of Western culture and continue to play a role in secular life. However, even as early as Plato, before the Judeo-Christian worldview permeated Western culture, philosophers were suspicious of an authoritarian deity—Plato raised a metaethical question of whether one's capacity to assert a moral authority actually justified one's moral principles as being right. Nevertheless, the assertion that moral principles reflect something essential about the nature of the Divine plays a critical role in *all* religions, as all religions hold specific moral positions that are attributed to the central divine figure and epitomized by this figure (or conception of this energy). In this fashion, not only does attributing moral principles (or justifying them) to a deity support the maintenance and authority of those moral principles in adherents, but they also communicate something essential about the very nature of the divine being inspiring these principles.

Another metaethic theory of moral principle may be defined **universalism.** Universalism suggests that moral principles are clearly defined and visible throughout the human community. Universalism itself does not imply a cause of morality, but rather asserts there are definable qualities of morality that are shared. We see this in the widely held incest taboo worldwide, whereby the majority human cultures overtly condemn incest. We also see universalism emerging in the general prohibition against murder (which is a culturally constructed action, meaning murder is defined by the culture—for example killing an "enemy combatant" does not necessarily equate to murder, however killing your neighbor for walking his dog on your lawn, does—these are defined by culture [a kind of hybrid of divine metaethic with a postmodern element, discussed shortly, overlaying universalism]). Universalism may manifest in a wide range of positions, such as *naturalism*—whereby moral principles are attributed to Nature and natural processes of life. More recently, they have been interpreted as intrapsychic in nature—such as a biological theory of morality, whereby humans are defined as the "moral animal". Under such interpretations moral principles are seen as developing due to evolutionary pressures.

Still another view of metaethics is the postmodern definition of **social construction** and social origin. These attributions state that principles of morality emerge only within the context of a given culture. They are literally social processes that serve to facilitate negotiation between the individual (self/ego) and the social others. Some suggest, as a socially constructed process, there can be no true moral principle except those reinforced by individuals with power. Thus an examination of any moral principle must also include an examination of power—on whose specific authority are *these* principles being made and what justifies their authority over one's own. The linkage with defining moral principles with power has played a critical role in the applied component of ethics, discussed momentarily. Further, the framing of ethics through social constructionism also reminds us that moral principles change. Moral principles become defined based on circumstances, history, power, cultural worldviews, etc. This differs from concepts of universalism and divinely inspired moral values that are seen as rooted and unchanging. Another way to consider this type of metaethic is **situational.**

In this capacity, we can essentially see metaethics as the process of asking not only where do moral principles emerge from, but under whose authority are these principles defined? And when asking under whose authority, why is *their* authority of more value than someone else's? As such, philosopher Geoff Sayre-McCord (2007), writes of metaethics: "Despite the abstract and deeply controversial nature of metaethics, its central concerns arise naturally—perhaps even inevitably—as one reflects critically on one's own moral convictions".[2] Thus metaethics asks us to ask deep questions of our moral convictions and their origin and justification.

Normative Ethics

Normative ethics refers to the process of labeling actions as morally right or wrong. The word *normative* has very specific implications that deserve exploring. First, normative implies there is a certain kind of universalism (whether restricted to a situation or broader cultural group of people or applied to *all* human beings) to ethics—all individuals can be measured against a normative ethical reference point. Second, normative ethics implies there are a well-defined right and wrong ways of action. What defines the right or wrong ultimately depends on the metaethics involved. For example, if one followed the US legal system's definition of normative ethics, stealing is wrong under all circumstances. If one utilized a different normative standard, perhaps one which holds the value that stealing food to feed one's family is the morally right choice, we have a different set of norms.

In our own social lives, we are often actively engaged in norms that emerge from situational metaethics. We operate at our work places based on workplace definitions of right and wrong and our own behavior is measured against workplace's defined norms. We accept (sometimes grudgingly) their ethical authority because of their social power, not necessarily their innate capacity to define right versus wrong. We also operate in our lives on religious ethics. Our behavior toward others through *all* situations seeks to be aligned to live up to what we perceive as the norms of behavior defined by our religious orientation (or another kind of potent normative standard). In this fashion, when we consider normative ethics, we are really asking *what* behaviors or actions are morally good or *right* or morally bad or *wrong*. This also includes **who has rights** and **who is privileged**, versus others who are seen as lacking rights, literally "wrong" or de-privileged. Who is essentially "right" *and thus* "good"? For example, any question that revolves around normative ethics might be: should nonhuman animals have equal rights as humans? This raises the issue of an *ought* or *should* (thus determining what is the norm), while at the same time conferring a certain moral description or condition onto an object of being (they are *right/good* because of who/what they are or represent). Finally, normative ethics are also visible in ethics codes or laws—whereby right and wrong are defined. If non-human animals are given the same rights as the human species, then nonhuman animals are considered "good" or *deserving of moral treatment.*

Before concluding, we need to look at the implied duality of this. Normative ethics are traditionally interpreted dualistically—there is a right as opposed to a wrong answer—it is either/or. This can oversimplify the challenges emergent within our complex society and as Neopagans, you'll immediately sense something erroneous in such a schism that ignores the holistic nature of life and our decision- making processes. In this capacity, normative ethics does require us to be cautious in our absoluteness—and to remain cognizant about when we determine an absolute good and an absolute bad—an all-good and an all-bad. When we make decisions about normative rights and wrongs, we need to be very clear as to the parameters of these determinations.

Applied Ethics

Applied ethics, as the name suggests, is the act of applying ethical considerations to situations to help resolve a situation. In short we call this **ethical decision making.** Throughout our lives we encounter situations where a defined right action may not be readily accessible. Not only might we not know what the *norm* is within a given situation (an ethically ambiguous situation), but we may not be able to decide what norm we should apply (whether to apply a norm derived from one metaethical position over another). When this situation occurs, we engage in decision-making processes.

Generally, when talking about applied ethics we are often referring to the process of engaging with complex and often controversial ethical issues, such as environmental ethics, animal rights, human rights, etc. Applied ethics takes ethical considerations out of the mental realm, the philosophical function, and into the practical and social realms. This helps us understand how viable and useful our ethics are—where do they fail to meet the challenges of a given situation and where do they help us determine a course of action. We may also see this application process as relating to our use of ethics codes. Often times, professions spend a great deal of time and resources developing ethics codes (normative ethics), but little time actually utilizing these codes to address issues within the profession.

Ethics within Religion

When we begin to explore the role of ethics within any religion, we are typically grounded in a divine metaethical framework that **states a basis for moral principles and moral action comes from some supernal power and authority**. This supernal power relates to us in a *perfect* and *absolute* correctness or rightness. This may or may not be specifically defined in normative terms. For example, some religious groups may see personally tragic or "bad" actions in their lives as essentially reflecting the good of the divine and a trust in the divine that all things have a purpose to the good outcome for the individual. Other religions may also develop a metaethic for "bad", attributing it to some demonic force. In this example, a normative view of the negative experiences in one's life may be attributed to the bad action of a supernal Bad; while all good actions in one's life are attributed to a supernal Good. Religions may also vary according to where the supernal power intercedes in human society and what situations (applied ethics) are to fall under the jurisdiction of the supernal power[3]. In this capacity, the first component of ethics in religion is the nature of the Supernal power that defines and epitomizes moral principle.

When we consider the **normative ethics of religion, we are referring to how adherents of a religion mirror/manifest/live the moral perfection of the Supernal power**. Thus normative ethics refer to how a religious organization and religious individuals define their norms as emergent from the Supernal power. In such a way, when a religion defines its moral codes, we can thus ask *why*. What are the metaethical reasons to support these ethical norms?

Finally, applied ethics serve to put into practice the norms defined by a religion. How are the norms **applied to a variety of situations**. For example, if one holds the ethical principle of harm none, how is this applied under a wide range of situations? One situation might define harm none as reflecting bodily harm; another emotional harm; still another might be setting a tough-love boundary—which may be perceived by the other as painful, but in the end is in their best interest. In which case, we can begin to see just how complex applied ethics can be. In the later chapters, we'll begin seeing how these issues apply specifically to Neopaganism.

Journal About It

In a journal, write Metaethics, Normative Ethics, and Applied Ethics on the top of three separate pages.

Under the Metaethics column, journal about your sources of ethics—where do you obtain information of right/wrong in your life. List all sources and next to each source describe your relationship to that source and spend time journaling about *why* that source has authority to set normative ethics for you.

On the next page, list all the norms that structure your behavior. At each one, jot down where these norms come from. Note any norms that you find unrealistic and any norms that might be in conflict with each other and lead challenge you if faced with a situation where you needed to choose between one norm over another.

On the final page, jot down how you act the norms you noted on the other page. Are their ones you really don't manifest in your everyday life? Which ones are the most challenging for you to live by and why and which are the easiest ones and why. Take your time to journal about this.

Finally on a fourth page, journal about what your own personal definition of ethics. What does Ethics mean for you and begin to speculate how ethics relates to Neopaganism.

2

Theological Ethics of Neopaganism Defined

Theological Ethics

> From a theological point of view, a moral ministry must be closely related to experiences of God and convictions about God. God is the ultimate center of value, the fixed point of reference for the morally right and wrong, the source and goal of all moral living.[1]

> Any ethical doctrine that makes theistic assumptions is theological.[2]

Theological ethics, regardless of religious origin, all share a common view: the ethics are derived and modeled after the Divine. Given this origin, theological ethics serve two central purposes: (a) illumination of the ultimate nature of the Divine, and (b) guidance on the best course of action for the adherent to be a manifestation/conduit of the Divine in their everyday life. Thus, contemplating the theological ethics of one's faith serves to enhance one's understanding of the nature of the Divine and how the Divine manifests in the world, while at the same time providing a model of behavior in the world. In this fashion, understanding the theological ethics of our religious choices allows us to *choose* when and how we manifest the Divine in our everyday lives. These choices in turn deepen our understanding of the nature of the Divine as we increase our direct experience of the Divine in our everyday behavioral and relational choices. Yet before we can model the Divine through our ethical choices, it's important to understand just how theological ethics illuminates the nature of the Divine and thus informs our behavioral choices.

Theological ethics illuminate three core elements of contemplation in the nature of the Divine:

(a) the ultimate *character* of the Divine (the Divine's "virtues");

(b) the *necessity* of the Divine (the irreplaceable role of the Divine in the maintaining life's processes); and

(c) the Divine's essential *perfection*.

All normative ethics that emerge from any religion derive from these three areas.

In **character** we find what constitutes essential moral Goodness. Contemplating this component of the Divine we are asking "how is the Divine 'Good'; what makes the Divine 'Virtuous'? What is the personality of the Divine?" When we contemplate **necessity**, we are looking at how the Divine is *required* in our existence, both at the micro (Personal/Soul level) and the macro (Family, Community, Cultural, Global, Natural levels). As such, we come to a deeper understanding of *how* and *where* and *when* the Divine enters into our immediate lives and the lives of humans and nonhumans alike. We are answering the question of "What are the undeniable moments of the Divine's presence in our existence?" In this fashion, the necessity of the Divine also reminds us that we are not alone and, as created beings of the Divine as well as illuminators of the Divine's presence in the world, we too are necessary. Finally, when we begin to contemplate the inherent **perfection** of the Divine, we begin to explore themes of purpose and justice—of how the Divine maintains the balance between freewill and destiny.

The Divine–Human Relationship

When we begin to engage in contemplation of the nature of the Divine *and* begin to apply the findings of these outcomes into our daily life, we enter into and illuminate a relationship between the Divine and ourselves. In this capacity, we can contemplate the nature of this relationship within the parameters of how the relationship manifests the character, necessity, and perfection of the Divine. It allows us to consider areas of personal growth—what circumstances in our lives challenge our capacity to manifest the virtues of the Divine, for example. What circumstances in our lives challenge our capacity to manifest perfection and necessity?

We call this process of contemplation and action **spiritual growth and striving**. Spiritual growth and striving is built upon the purpose of increasing closeness between ourselves and the Divine through increasing awareness of our own Divine Nature. In fact all religious traditions hold at their core the concept of *becoming like the Divine* or *merging with the Divine* or *transcending the human–Cultural environments to become One with the Divine*. A core belief in all religions holds the human soul is Divine and through contemplation we can begin to awaken this state in our earthly existence[3]. From this perspective, theological ethics become the prescription for how to spiritually grow.

Deontology

A final word on theological ethics, particularly as they differ from the field of ethics: deontology and voluntarism. These are two principles that typically emerge within theological ethics to varying degrees of focus specific to each religion. Voluntarism refers to what we know as **Divine Command Ethics,** which falls under the broader category of Deontology, the title of our section. **Deontology** is comprised of three parts: (a) moral obligation or requirement; (b) moral rightness (prescription/permission to act a certain way); and (c) moral prohibition (proscription/being forbidden to act a certain way).

> **Moral obligation** essentially means commands by the Divine and the degree to which we volunteer or choose to follow them (*voluntarism*). In this way, we are required by our Divine being to act in a certain way in order to retain our connection to and manifest the Nature of the Divine in our lives. These are often the specific and accepted *laws* of any faith's ethical requirements. They are often the underlying tenants of a faith, for example we see in Neopagan traditions the underlying law, *harm none*. This is not a choice, but a command, we are told to harm none and only then do as we wish. In Judeo–Christian traditions, we find the Decalogue (the ten commandments), whereby ten specific behavioral actions are outlined as necessary if the adherent is to keep in good grace with the Divine. In short, all religions have explicit (overtly spelled out, often through religious texts) or implicit (implied) commands that are *required* for the adherent to do in order to *relate* to the Divine.
>
> **Moral rightness** has some diverse interpretations and meanings depending on the religion, but in general moral rightness refers to behaviors that are either (a) *not* explicitly prohibited and thus may be engaged in without Divine consequence; OR (b) they are behaviors that the adherent interprets as implied/condoned by Divine command—in this capacity the Divine command is theologically reasoned to extend to include a set of behaviors that are similar to overtly stated ones but not explicitly noted. In Moral Rightness, we also have the issue of choice. We are asked to decide which behaviors are permissible because they are essentially in line with the moral commands. This component can be a source of ethical challenge in that it requires interpretation. For example, Jesus cautions his adherents that what they do to the least they do to him. This is not an explicit command that requires adherents to

treat those with less or those who are viewed with less social power, with respect, love, and support. Instead it is open to interpretation. It requires theological interpretation as to who Jesus meant when he said "less". While logic might hold that the morally right behavior based on the commands of Jesus would be to treat all with respect, etc., theologians may wiggle out of this by interpreting this statement to include only those who share the same Christian tradition who may be disadvantaged. This may then fail to constrain harmful behaviors engaged in between Christian groups or between a Christian group and another religious, ethnic, or cultural group, as theologians may define "least" as within-group (that is only within the Christian group) and thus retain a theological belief that all others are exempt from morally right treatment.

Moral prohibitions are behaviors that are either explicitly or implicitly held to be morally wrong. They can reflect either the opposition of a Divine command. For example, within Neopagan ethics there is the underlying command to live in concert with Nature and its cycles. If we do not engage in this command, then we are essentially engaging in morally prohibited behavior. Additionally, we may determine moral prohibition based on extrapolating upon a command. For example, the Hebrew Scriptures hold one is not to kill. If one maintains an environmentally centered Jewish faith, they may interpret this prohibition to extend to the eating of nonhuman animals—thus the prohibition supports a morally right position of vegetarianism within the context of a theological framework. As such our moral prohibitions may emerge from (a) our own interpretations a divine commandment, extending it to other facets of life, OR (b) to explicitly stating the opposite of a moral prescription in a Divine Command. Similar to the challenge raised by moral rightness, moral prohibition runs the risk of demonstrating bias through theological interpretation that can bring about harm to others.

These three elements are important to explore when examining the ethical framework of one's faith. In particular it is critical to pay close attention to prohibition and rightness as these typically require our own interpretation. We need to pay close attention to how our interpretations impact those around us, particularly those who do not share our own faith; how we treat others of different faiths is itself an ethical issue that must be identified, articulated, and engaged in. Or to rephrase this, in order to engage in responsible theological framing it is critical for the theologian to assess their own cultural frames of reference for bias (in other words look for areas where one's own blinders about what is true about the world and those within it could foster neglectful, harmful, or discriminatory action). We'll be returning to this specific issue when we come to ethical decision making.

Neopagan Ethics Defined

Introduction

Neopaganism is uniquely different from all other clusters of religious paths in that the underlying faiths associated with this broad path generally do not follow any dogmatic or universally revealed text of a Divine being. Rather faith traditions typically emerge through oral exchange between social groups and through individual interpretations that emerge based on a wide range of reading materials available that seek to define what Wicca, Goddess, Druidic, and other paths are. While there have been a few texts focused on ethics within the Neopagan faith, such as *An Ye Harm None: Magical Morality and Modern Ethics* by Shelly TSivia Rabinovitch and Meredith Macdonald and *Living with Honor: A Pagan Ethics* by Emma Restall Orr, articulating core ethical statements of Neopaganism can be challenging due to the very individual nature of the theology of Neopaganism that holds that each individual reveals the nature of the Divine, and as such each individual's interpretation of the Divine holds value. This can mean that within Neopaganism there can be a wide range of ethical articulations to explore. For example, Orr writes:

> In order to ensure my definition [of ethics] grounded, on a number of occasions throughout the past few years I have asked gatherings of Pagans to help unpack the terms that readily surround *ethics*. It is the results of these discussion that I have used as a guide here: definitions crafted by thinking people, seeking a collective clarity about how the words are used in the realities of everyday life and language in our Western culture.
>
> Here is the first definition, derived from these gatherings. *Ethics:* the line we draw that articulates what is acceptable in terms of behaviour, and what is not, from a profoundly personal and individual standpoint.
>
> Putting aside any notion about where the line *should* be, more basically our ethics are an expression of our needs. Bluntly, they declare what we feel the world owes us and what we feel we ought to give in return. Our ethics describe how we feel others ought to conduct their lives and how we sense we too ought to behave. Based entirely on the patterns of our own minds,

they reflect how we perceive the world, both in terms of the *facts* we assume are reality, and the emotionally defended attitudes that we *believe* and often *need* to be true. Just as these beliefs shape how we respond to the world, so do they create the ethical framework of standards and expectations that we use to judge ourselves and others: the line of what is acceptable, what is forgivable. As such, our ethics provoke guilt and anger, shame, gratitude and humility, compassion and lack of mercy, a sense of injustice and righteousness. Where the line is crossed, we find fear and grief. Where we hold inflexibly, it becomes a cloak that keeps us comforted, armour that keeps us safe, clear air that keeps us healthy. Here is the framework within which we think.[4]

There are two central issues that are worth noting in Orr's discussion as it pertains to Neopagan ethics. First the definition of theological ethics emerges within a communal discussion, the direct and explicit sharing and transmitting of ideas between groups and individuals. As noted this is markedly different from other religions whereby ethics are codified and made explicit through a commonly accepted text (or several core texts such as in the case of Buddhism and Hinduism). In this capacity, we must first note the ethics of Neopaganism remain essentially fluid. While I will soon attempt to delineate a few core ethics widely accepted, this list cannot be seen as a universally revealed doctrine or divine command.

The second aspect that warrants note is Orr's definition of Neopagan ethics as one that describes how the individual adherents interpret the world and what they feel is morally right or wrong. This, too, is centrally different from other religious traditions whereby the original intuiters of a Divine ethic are either lost to history or deified themselves, thus viewed as the *only* acceptable conduits to teaching the Divine Command Ethics to humankind. What we see in Neopaganism is that ethics emerge in the diverse traditions based on the coming together of individual senses of right and wrong. In Orr's interpretation there is little divine about this development and as such it could be argued that she is not defining theological ethics, but is more focused toward cultural–social ethics. In this capacity Orr is not exploring Neopaganism as a religion, but rather as a cultural lifestyle. Nevertheless, we can in fact gain an important insight into the theological nature of Neopagan ethics—*all* individuals are conduits for the Divine Commands.

This draws upon the central tenant of Neopagan traditions that each individual is a manifestation of the Divine—the divine is *both* immanent and eminent—both manifesting within us and acting outside of us. As such, the privileging of the individual ethical definition and interpretation of the world *does reveal a theological ethic*—an ethic of the Divine. In this fashion, Neopagans do not simply contemplate the nature of the Divine as if it were an abstract, but hold that they must *awaken* the nature of the divine within themselves and thus manifest the character, necessity, and perfection of the Divine in their everyday life. This is the central core concept of ethics in Neopaganism. And it may be worth considering as ethics in Neopaganism are *living*, fluid, reactive, and changing based on the growth and movement of life, they inherently reflect a conception of the Divine's nature as one that is ever-changing and growing.

The Divine in Neopaganism: Character, Necessity, & Perfection

Before we can specifically discuss the core ethics of Neopaganism, we need to take a moment to discuss the Divine in Neopaganism, which ultimately gives rise to and roots the ethics. First and foremost Neopagan traditions vary widely across three broad concepts of the Divine: henotheism, polytheisim, and pantheism. Most Neopagans are **henotheistic**, whereby they believe in the existence of multiple Divine beings, but often focus their attention on one Deity at a given time (a patron or a Deity that is most beneficial for a specific ritual or goal). Neopagans that are truly **polytheistic** believe and engage with multiple Deities simultaneously; for example Wiccans who engage with the Lord *and* Lady in ritual work, view the world as containing a Divine Female and Male energy (which may or not be reflected in a specific named Divine being known from earlier polytheistic religious traditions). Neopagans that are **pantheistic** hold a belief in an ultimate divine being who reveals itself through the world at large—is found everywhere and in everything living being and in the created universe, and all other divine beings are seen as simply a reflection of this central essence. It is uniquely different from monotheism in that the divine being cannot be described by humanlike qualities or is delimited in space (monotheism rejects true pantheism and holds the singular God or Goddess is spatially outside of the physical realm). Each of these core understandings of the Divine nature carry with them personal conceptualizations of the nature of the Divine being.

In a henotheistic and a polytheistic framework, the Divine beings often take on very tangible humanlike character traits that are often revealed through mythic storytelling and ritual channeling. In pantheistic beliefs the divine is not revealed solely through a humanlike deity, but may be defined through processes in Nature and visible in other species. Pantheism is most widely seen in shamanistic Neopagan traditions whereby the natural world *is* the Divine and ethics are linked to what Nature reveals about the fundamentals of life. Let's look at an example of Neopagan henotheism: Dianic Witchcraft.

Dianic Witchcraft is a henotheistic tradition that centrally figures the Virgin

Goddess of the Hunt, Diana/Artemis. It is henotheistic in that most Dianic Witches, while viewing Diana as the patron of the faith itself, other Goddesses may take their turn in ritual focus depending on the needs of the adherent. However, Diana, as a central patron, has very specific virtues: she is *virginal* (ultimately meaning sexually empowered, autonomous, and unattached—not a literal virgin); she is the *protectress* of the wilds and childbirth; she is *bringer* of sustenance/fruitfulness. As with all religions, the virtues of the Divine being associated with that faith serve to define the core values of the faith. In the case of Dianic Witchcraft, the virtues of Diana are interpreted as the following virtues:

> To remain virginal does not equate to sexual chastity, but with autonomy, independence, and sexual and female empowerment. This specific virtue of Diana also served to provide an ideal Divinity for the Lesbian community, whereby worth and value could be achieved outside of a heterosexual lifestyle. As the movement expanded and interacted with broader feminist principles and groups of women, the virtue of virginity came to mean the necessity and right of independent female power. Thus Dianic Witches often hold feminist ethical beliefs that can be thealogical linked to the fundamental sexual independence of Diana.
>
> To be a protectress of infants, mothers, and the wild spaces holds Diana's centrality in the cycle of life, particularly overseeing the maiden aspects of this cycle. The virtue is also a feminist ethic. It refers to the capacity to ensure the well-being and health of those seen as less-than men—those who are relegated to a position of less authority within a patriarchal society. Thus the Dianic Witch takes an active role in protecting through public and private life, through religious and mundane life, the integrity of those who have less social power in our society. In this fashion, the protectress reflects the virtue of caring for the least in society and empowering them, including Nature itself.
>
> The final virtue that emerges in the Goddess Diana is that of the sustainer, the one who brings nourishment through her oversight of the hunt. Because Diana oversees the wild places, She holds a special relationship with nonhuman animals that may be a food source. It is only through Her intercession is a hunt successful (which is also linked to shamanistic practices). Yet Diana, as protectress, means that She has an obligation to preserve life of the wild ones. Thus to be the sustainer means to also be a balancer—to ensure that no more than what is truly needed is given. Thus she sustains through engaging in sustainability. In

Dianic Witchcraft this often emerges in the drive of engaging in responsible, environmental action—supporting sustainability and moderation—recognizing that all of life is interconnected, for Diana is both the Taker/Giver of Life—through Her the balance of life is sustained.

In this example, abbreviated though it is, we can see the relationship between the character of the Divine being and how this influences the ethical values of the specific Neopagan tradition. We can remain with this Neopagan tradition as an example to illustrate how necessity and perfection emerge.

Dianic Witchcraft holds that Diana is a *necessary* being in the existence of life; it is from her energy that life remains in balance. Her virtues are not merely models for human behavior, but reflect core functions of the universe itself. Diana is the energy of choice[5], specifically the choice to reject something—all living beings have this instilled in them despite how restrictively we may interpret instinct. Diana is also the universal energy that expends a great deal of time ensuring that living beings survive and thrive—thus the infant survival rates exceed the losses to ensure species continue. Diana is also a universal balancer—while ensuring survival, she also ensures limitation and control—not all living beings will survive, some will feed others and thus whole populations are kept in balance with others. Life itself becomes sustainable through Diana. Mythologically and thealogically Diana is viewed as necessary, essential.

When we conceptualize *perfection* and Diana, we hold that these virtues and cycles of necessity manifest in Diana as untarnished and perfect. As a divine being, She makes no mistakes and we in turn trust in Her perfection. She embodies the perfect model of how to act in the world. When we engage in the world, modeled after her, we in turn experience some of her perfection.

As we wrestle with character, necessity, and perfection elements of the Deity conception we work with, we begin to have a fuller more complete understanding of our own theological underpinnings of the Neopagan tradition we practice and will someday become a priest/ess of. Some critical beginning questions to ask yourself are:

1. What are the character traits of the Divine being(s) who guide me and how do these inform what I do and how I see the world?

2. We must also ask qualitatively how deep and mutual our relationship is with the Divine. One important question to consider is: Do I see the Divine being(s) as servants to *my* goals and will (thus I only communi-

cate with them when I need something) or do I see this being as the source of my goals and lifestyle choices?

3. Theological ethics and pastoral leadership requires us to examine the specific nature of the Divine and its relationship to the broader aspects of life, thus extending the discussion outside our individual selves and needs. Another way to think of this is to remember the core element of Neopaganism: Immanence and Eminence. While each of us manifests the Divine, the Divine is simultaneously a core, universal aspect of a totality (whether you believe in One central being or multiple beings that collectively create the universe in its totality)—this is the eminent nature of the Divine. It is beyond any single person—any single, individual revelation. If we restrict our understanding to what is within us and our own needs, then we are operating with only one eye and as such we will miss the wider picture. As such, we can ask, what other visions contribute to my understanding of the Divine?

Core Ethics

In this section, we'll look at core, nearly universal Neopagan ethics and how they can be defined and understood at the theological level through their implications for metaethics, normative ethics, and applied ethics. It's important to keep in mind that this list is not complete as each tradition of Neopaganism often has its own set of ethics, further these ethics often emerge from the conceptions of the Divine that inform that tradition, and there is still further variability *between* individuals who intuit the parameters of ethics.

Do as you wish, as long as it harms none

This is a command ethic in most Neopagan traditions. While no deity is ultimately attributed to charging adherents with the command to harm none (most interpret it as the Goddess), it is a largely universal ethic to all religions. It also resonates within a Western cultural tradition that values individual freedom. This ensures that we respect the rights of others, while at the same time also respecting our own goals. If we look closely though at this ethic we find there are actually two ethics embedded: the command to harm none and the command to do as one wishes. Thus, in Neopaganism the conception of this ultimate ethic is that the Divine being wants us to live our lives authentically based on what we desire, but at the same time remain conscious of others and responsible to others to ensure that we do not overstep our own parameters.

Metaethic element: this ethic has no named Divine origin, but assumes that the underlying principle in life is to facilitate our own personal needs, while being constrained so as not to step on those of others. In this fashion, this ethic assumes a fundamental belief in the rights of each living being to pursue their interests without infringing upon others. It is in essence the true meaning of freedom that ensures all individuals in life remain respected. Related to this ethic is the Karmic law that holds a fundamental element of Nature is that whatever action you take, good or bad/right or wrong, will return to you—thus it remains best to be responsible and thoughtful.

Normative element: this ethic makes an explicit statement of right and wrong behavior. We are permitted to do anything we wish providing we do not bring harm to others through our choices. Thus it establishes a norm that reminds us to keep aware of the impact of our actions on others—establishing personal responsibility. However, it is important to note that this ethic is also very ambiguous—what does harm mean and can we seek out too many desires, thus overconsume or become hedonistic? In this capacity, we arrive at the applied element.

Applied element: this ethic demands of us to be aware of how we theologically interpret the norms established—what does it mean to do anything we wish, what are the limits of this if any, should there be limits? What does harm mean? Are their situations where harm may come to others, but it is necessary? How do we apply this ethic in our lives and how do situations impact how we apply this ethic?

Every living being is a reflection of the Divine

In Neopaganism there is a fundamental belief that each individual reflects the Divine—as such there is a privileging of every voice, ideally, in a given Neopagan tradition. We may see this as the fundamental sacredness of *all* life. We seek out information from others and often incorporate diverse perspectives into our own crafting of our beliefs. We respect the unique intuitions and revelations of others as conveying important elements of our faith and we also hold that all other living beings convey something essential of the Divine as well. Thus all individuals deserve our respect.

Metaethic element: here again there is no one myth that is suggestive of this immanent/eminent nature of our relationship to the Divine, but it centrally holds an underlying process of the universe is the fundamental interconnectedness between all living beings and the divine. This gives rise to the mythos, stories, and views of a sacred "web of life".

Normative element: this ethic establishes the fundamental behavior of respect for difference and the capacity to look for the Divine in all living things.

Thus right behavior is one's capacity to remain open and respectful of all others, while wrong behavior would be seen as a violation of this drive of openness and respect for difference. As such prejudice, bias, and so forth would be seen as behaviors that reflect violations of this ethic.

Applied element: When we consider how we apply this ethic in our everyday life we are really being challenged to assess the degree to which we remain open to others and respectful of their own voices. It also raises a particular ethical challenge of under what circumstance must we engage in debate and challenge the views and practices of others. There is a risk for interpreting this ethic in an ethically diluted way that holds all actions, all views, etc. are a manifestation of the Divine and thus no one should dispute them. This is a risky position to hold since it potentially leads to remaining socially and politically inert in the face of very harmful actions, such as genocide or ecocide or extinction. Thus we must interpret this ethic within the primary ethic of do no harm—as such if we see harm, if we *do nothing* we are essentially engaging in harming behavior and thus violating the primary ethic of Neopaganism. As such, it is important to recognize that this ethic does not state ALL actions of individuals are reflections of the Divine; rather we remain open to hear what others have to say and to evaluate whether these statements and behaviors really could reflect the Divine.

The Earth is sacred

Neopagan traditions are universally steeped in ritual life that connects the individual to Nature, whereby Nature is seen as Divine.

Metaethic element: Different traditions view Nature subtly different. Some traditions see Nature, like other elements of life *as created by* the divine and therefore deserving of respect. Some traditions hold Nature *is* Divine and exhibits a central aspects of the Divine, as such Nature is deserving of not only respect but worship.

Normative element: Regardless of the underlying metaethic orientation, both centrally hold that the protection and preservation of Nature and the respect for Nature's essential right to exist are held as morally right behaviors.

Applied element: When we look to applying this ethic in behavior we can look at our own behavioral relationship to Nature, such as recycling or activism. For example the Reclamation Movement of Wicca is rooted in environmental action as a core behavior.

Joyfulness, creativity, and pleasure are Divine

Neopagan traditions all embrace individual creativity, joy and pleasure. Many traditions, such as Wiccan ones, overtly state that the acts of joy and pleasure are the literal acts of the Goddess, thus to seek joy, pleasure and to create is to honor the Goddess.

Metaethic element: In both Druidism and Celtic Wicca, there are deities that are revered specifically for their creative capacities—both procreative and artistically creative. While in other traditions of Wicca, the Goddess, known by all names, mandates us to seek joy and pleasure. In each case, built into the processes of all life is the capacity to create (biologically or creatively) and to seek out joy.

Normative element: There is an interesting normative view of Neopaganism that separates itself from just about all other faiths. It holds that it is normal or right to feel joy and thus not suffer. In this capacity suffering is viewed as incongruent with the Divine. This is also why many Neopagans hold beliefs such as disease reflects "dis-ease", something out of balance, something out of sync; as well as holding beliefs that one can thus heal suffering, whether physical or emotional or relational, through rebalancing oneself toward the Divine through ritual healing, prayer, or magic for example.

Applied element: One of the ways we see this ethic manifest in behavior is the actual fluidity of Neopagan traditions themselves and their readiness to embrace new ritual formats and to encourage creative spontaneity. There is also the drive of many Neopagans to express themselves in creative projects ranging from the crafting of one's own ritual tools to jewelry to writing to artwork to music. In Druidism there is the Bardic tradition which is associated with poetry. We may also apply this framework to creatively solve problems and explore new solutions; to reject stagnation and embrace change.

Activity

Take a moment now to journal about the above broad ethics and consider how they relate to your own Neopagan path and write down how they manifest in your everyday life. Consider what challenges you face in manifesting the ethics as well and what in your faith provides the theological framework for the ethics. Then spend some time writing down any additional ethics that are associated with your own Neopagan path. Consider the following:
1. the Divine/Theological origin of the ethic—where does it come from;
2. the underlying norms of the ethic (right/wrong);
3. and how this ethic is applied in situations; and
4. how do you see this ethic emerging in your everyday life.

3
Character & Worldview of the Priest/ess

Worldview & Value Orientations

> Each of us possesses a worldview that affects how we perceive and evaluate situations and how we derive appropriate actions based on our appraisal...[1]

> ...neopagans must approach everything and everyone they encounter with the same level of respect that they show to other, more explicit, expressions of divinity.[2]

> values, *Sociology*. the ideals, customs, institutions, etc., of a society toward which the people of the group have an affective regard. These values may be positive, as cleanliness, freedom, or education, or negative, as cruelty, crime, or blasphemy.[3]

In 1961 two anthropologists Kluckhohn and Strodtbeck published a text entitled *Variations in Values Orientations*. Based on extensive research cross-culturally, Kluckhohn and Strodtbeck identified five core problems that individuals and cultures grapple with in association with human existence:

(a) Time: what is the temporal focus in life?;

(b) Human Nature: What is the character of innate human nature?;

(c) Relational: What is the basis for human relationships with other humans?;

(d) Activity: What is the basis for human activity?; and

(e) Person–Nature–Supernature: What is the relationship between humanity and Nature and Supernature?.[4]

As cultures and individuals grapple with these core questions, they do so through the development of sustained values, which in turn collectively comes to create their worldview. Further, individuals differ from the broader cultures in that when they come to personally grapple with these five questions, they often maintain all the possible value orientations associated with that problem; whereas the broader culture typically manifest one central value orientation (the dominant value). In the Table 3.1 are the value orientations that individuals and cultures select from when looking to address the broad issues of human existence. When we examine the value orientations to critical questions about our existence, it's important to recognize that we do not necessarily fall into any one category neatly. Rather we can look at the possible answers to each of these existential questions on a continuum. And many times, the diverse social groups that have meaning in our lives will differ uniquely along these values.

For example, if you live in Western society (a broad social group affiliation) and are Neopagan (a smaller social group affiliation) you'll likely find yourself facing a choice in values and may even struggle with maintaining a sense of *internal values consistency* across social contexts—that is you may find yourself feeling torn and often having to adopt conflicting values in different social situations, leaving you feeling less than positive about yourself and perhaps even confused about what you believe in and what's important. Western society (European and White Americans largely) as a whole tends to hold the values: future, mixed, individualism (often referred to as "rugged"), doing, and control/dominating nature[5]. In contrast, a Neopagan value system tends to be fluid, mixed[6], web, being-in-becoming, and harmony (we'll talk about this in greater depth in a moment). In this fashion, the contemporary Neopagan adherent often faces the challenge of living in a culture that is markedly different from their underlying spiritual understanding of how the universe functions and what is important to them personally.

We typically negotiate these cultural–values conflicts through the maintenance of *fluid social identities*. These fluid social identities are flexible views of ourselves that we deploy in various situations. This aids us in reducing **cognitive dissonance**. Cognitive dissonance is an internally distressing experience that emerges when our internal beliefs or behaviors are in conflict with the larger social group. When this occurs most people typically adopt the group's beliefs or behaviors and rationalize this adoption in a positive light to reduce any personal feelings of guilt, shame, distress that occurs when we forgo our own internal beliefs. Cognitive dissonance may also occur internally between two conflicting ideas—whereby we look for external information to help us choose which idea

Character & Worldview of the Priest/ess

Time	Human Nature	Relational	Activity	Person–Nature
Past — Focus on past events	Bad — Human nature is essentially evil	Individual — Emphasis on autonomy and personal needs	Being — Spontaneous expression of self through action—"just be"	Subjugation — Individuals are subjugated by Nature and have no control—people cannot change their essential natures.
Present — Focus is on the present moment	Mixed — Human nature has the potentiality of good and bad—the emphasis is on personal choice and may include an awareness of the impact of environment on behavior.	Collateral — Emphasis is focused on how actions impact an extended social network located in the present moment.	Becoming — Focus is on personal growth and development	Harmony — Individuals should live in harmony with Nature and forces outside of Nature.
Future — A focus on future potentials, attention directed to what may come rather than what is. Can lead to a belief that tomorrow is better than today	Good — Humans are essentially good	Lineal — Emphasis is placed on ancestral relationships and the maintenance of social order through time—how one's actions fit within both the present and historical elements of one's social connections	Doing — Focus is placed on achievement-oriented activities based on externally set standards, rather than self-growth standards	Control — Individuals believe they can manipulate, control, change, dominate forces and elements of Nature.
Fluid¹ — A view that time is not fixed but the past, present, and future are all viewed as important lens.	Neutral–Ambivalent — Human nature is neither good, bad, or mixed—it exists in potentiality or little emphasis is placed on understanding the nature of human beings.	Web¹ — Emphasis is placed on a view relationships extend into the past and outward to incorporate nonhuman species and environment as a relational being	Being-in-Becoming — This blends both the capacity to engage in spontaneous action and how these form a foundation for personal development.	

Table 5.1

is the better one to maintain and provide us with a reason to justify the rejection of the other. When we begin to explore ethical dilemmas, we'll be returning to this topic as most ethical dilemmas create cognitive dissonance and many stem from discrepancies between our diverse social identities and their cultural value affiliations.

When we turn our direction from the Neopagan adherent to the Neopagan priest and priestess, we encounter a central challenge of being a priest and priestess. In short, we "judge the effectiveness of ministers in terms of the congruence of their beliefs, personal life, and performance"[9] with the theo/alogical principles of their tradition. In this fashion, adherents look to their priests and priestesses as models of how to negotiate contemporary life through the *maintenance* of the core values of their religious tradition. Given the marked difference, indeed *opposition*, between Neopagan core value orientations with the majority Western culture, the issue of consistency and congruency becomes one of the most challenging issues facing Neopagan priests and priestesses. As such, one of the most important skills the priest and priestess gain is their capacity to cultivate an awareness of the value orientations of **all** their primary social environments they actively negotiate (this includes their primary family, extended family, work environments [if Priest/Priestess is not their primary occupation], school environments, friendships, town, state, and country affiliations). This examination means the priest/ess understands how each of their social group affiliations resolve the five central problems noted in Table 3-1. Once there is the awareness of the underlying values orientations all their social groups have, the priest/ess has an opportunity to determine situations where they will experience the greatest amount of difficulty with maintaining their dominant core value orientation (ideally the Neopagan one) and brainstorm ideas on how to increase congruency.

Activity 1: Defining Your Social Identity Values

We are all members of diverse groups and each of these groups has a unique way of understanding the world around them. Some groups, particularly those containing members we have strong emotional connections too, play a significant role in how we will come to see the world and privilege that group's specific way of seeing the world over other ways of seeing. Other groups have less emotional saliency to us and we typically feel little pressure to mirror (be congruent with) their values. As noted above, when we consider the role of becoming a priest/ess it is critical to understand and unpack the very salient groups we exist within to identify sources of potential conflict between the values of that group and our religious identity values. In this activity, do the following:

1. Identify all the diverse social groups you are a member of.

2. Next to each group, note the degree to which this group is important to (a) your self-concept (how you see yourself; what you *think* about yourself); (b) your emotional well-being (how you *feel* about yourself or about events in your life; for example, while many individuals say work is "just a job" many experience marked emotional impacts from work, signifying work is often much more than this); and (c) your behavioral choices (how you *act* in the world; what decisions you make).

3. Identify how each group orients itself according to Table 3-1.

4. Identify any sources of *actual* or *potential* values conflicts between your different groups—for example, say your work environment follows a strict hierarchical structure and those in charge often demean those beneath them (Controlling and Lineal values), while a majority of your other social groups value cooperation and egalitarian structures (Web and Harmony).

5. Take time to write about how you respond to these conflicts—some questions to ask yourself: do you stay in the social group and ignore the conflict? Do you attempt to change the social group to bring it into greater consistency with how you feel? Do you leave the social group?

Activity 2: Clarifying Neopagan Values

In this activity you'll have an opportunity to define your Neopagan values orientation in depth. To do this you'll need paper and a pen (or better a journal that you designate strictly for your Ethics work). You'll need at least five pages, at the top of each page write one of the five values question headings: Time, Human Nature, Relational, Activity, and Person–Nature interaction. Take time to identify how your spiritual beliefs are organized in the possible values orientations under each of the five central values questions. Generally, Neopaganism follows a Fluid, Mixed, Web, Being-in-Becoming, and Harmony core value system; however your own personal orientation may differ slightly. Once you've done this, begin to explore and journal about how you manifest each of the core values. For example, you may wish to consider ethics such as "the sacredness of the earth" to expound upon the notion of harmony. You wish to consider the issue of karma in terms of a fluid time structure and how this impacts your understanding of the world around you. You may also find that there is overlap between the various core values and that that they interact with one another. The following elements should be explored in your written contemplations:

1. Behavioral and lifestyle examples of the values orientations—how you *do* the values in everyday life;

2. Theo/alogical and/or ethical examples of the values orientations—how does your understanding of the Divine impact the creation of values;

3. Ritual examples of the value orientations—how do you interpret these values within your ritual life;

4. Emotional reactions to the values orientations—how do you *feel* about these values.

Activity 3: Defining Your Worldview

Your worldview is a succinct description of the lens from which you see the world around you. Worldviews are comprehensive integrations of how our value orientations interact both with each other and with our social identities (the roles we play in diverse social groups); yet it also suggests our underlying sense of cosmology (how we see the universe functions). In this capacity, the worldview is not solely the sum total of our core values, but also our underlying beliefs about the "whys" of the universe. And most of us—whether we aware of it or not—formulate an essential answer to the issue of how the universe works and our relationship to the ultimate question. This may be a position of atheism, whereby there is an outright rejection of the existence of a divine force or a theistic position (such as a Neopagan position would hold), whereby there is a divine force at work in the world. Our view of *how* and *why* of the world, our unique way of "seeing" the world around us that determines our behaviors in and reactions to the world around us. As an individual exploring the potentiality of becoming a Neopagan priest/ess or as someone who already maintains this position, it is important to define what your worldview is *and* how this relates to your definition of what you feel defines a *Neopagan* worldview at large.

In this activity, take some time to articulate your own worldview. I generally recommend you allow yourself to free write and do not limit how much you write. Once you are done, review what you have written and come up with a three sentence description beginning with *How I see the world…* You can include your core values from the previous exercises as well. Once you have this done, take time to write about what the Neopagan worldview is—utilize texts, the internet, and your own experiences to brainstorm various elements of this worldview. Read over these statements and come up with a three sentence worldview defining Neopaganism. Once this is done, take a moment to examine how your personal worldview relates to the broader Neopagan worldview—how are they similar? In what ways do they differ? Are there any marked areas of difference that could create a conflict between your role as a priest/ess in a Neopagan tradition and your personal vision?

Character

When we begin to talk about character, we're talking about psychological elements of personal goals, our attitudes, and general dispositional traits that coalesce to form a cohesive character or sense of a person within a given social role. What defines whether a character trait is "good" or "bad" largely depends on the social situation the character trait is deployed. For example, if someone has a tendency toward thrill-seeking, risk-taking and a disregard for personal safety and is a participant in extreme sports or firefighting, we wouldn't consider these character traits as "bad". However, we might consider these traits as unhealthy if they occur outside of a social environment where they are beneficial. At the same time, if someone is meticulous, detail-oriented, and follows strict plans they might do very well as a researcher, but these same traits might be a mismatch within a social environment that is unstructured. When we think about character we are thinking about **fit** between ourselves and the social environment we are looking to engage with. When we apply this to the social–occupational role of the Neopagan priest and priestess, we are looking at the degree of fit between our (a) personal goals and values (motivation–intention), (b) our attitudes (how we feel about something), and (c) our general disposition (a tendency to act a certain way) and the requirements of the role of priest/ess. As such this requires not only the capacity for us to define our own personal character, but to consider it in relation to what the character of a Priest/ess is.

The Association of Theological Schools in the United States and Canada[10] began a long-term study[11] on what qualities are desirable and problematic in individuals entering into a ministerial position. In their research three characterological traits were found to be most desirable: (a) service without need for public recognition; (b) integrity; and (c) generosity. In this fashion, to be a minister an individual must have an underlying motivation for service without the need for public recognition—in other words, service for service sake. Integrity reflects the capacity for an individual to keep their word and maintain consistency; while generosity refers to our capacity to be open and giving of self to others. What this study illustrates is the primary ethics of a minister have little to do with knowledge, education, leadership skills and a great deal more to do with having and being able to maintain personal ethics. In contrast, the study found the three most undesirable traits were defined as: (a) lack of disciple; (b) self-serving; and (c) immaturity. A lack of discipline reflected not only a lifestyle of excess, but also disorganization in one's personal life, emotions, and environments. While self-serving reflects an individual who places their own needs above the needs of their coven or congregation and structures the role of priest/ess to solely serve one's ego rather than to serve the Divine energy that guides the specific tradition the individual speaks for. Finally, immaturity reflects an inability: (a) to maintain a leadership position, (b) to manifest the breadth and scope of the religious ethics of the specific tradition, and (c) to manifest depth in theological thinking. Considering this study we can develop a preliminary description of the ideal character of a priest/ess, as follows:

1. motivated for service, both to adherents and to the divinity of the tradition;

2. maintains an attitude of respect and integrity—behaviorally manifesting the ethic all are divine ("thou art goddess"; "an it harm none" for example);

3. maintains an attitude of generosity, authenticity, and openness;

4. is disciplined, organized, and focused in behavior, thought, and emotional response;

5. is empathic and sympathetic—oriented to fully *hearing* others;

6. motivated for personal growth and deepening one's knowledge and relationship to the divine;

7. maintains congruency between faith and behavior, "as above, so below; as within, so without";

8. has a mature religious identity; this means the individual feels certain in their beliefs and does not feel threatened by other religious beliefs and is able to translate their beliefs into their everyday behavior.

Activity 1: Virtue in Action

Virtues are distilled from core values of a social environment. They reflect a standard or normative ethic of what is a "good" character trait to ensure the well-being of the specific community. When we apply this to Neopaganism we are looking at the types of virtues that are supported within the faiths and thus *should* be modeled by the priest/esses of those traditions. Some core virtues seen in Neopaganism:

> Balance
> Holism
> Diversity
> Compassion/Empathy/Sympathy
> Creativity
> Fairness
> Cooperativeness
> Joyfulness
> Self-awareness
> Openness
> Reverence
> Responsibility
> Generosity
> Fidelity—"perfect trust"
> Loving Kindness—"perfect love"

Take time to write about how you manifest each of these virtues in your life *outside* of times designated as clearly religious in nature. Consider how you personally define these virtues and why they are important within Neopaganism; additionally consider what challenges you experience in always manifesting these. Finally, consider your specific Neopagan drives, whether toward Goddess-based path, a Wiccan-based path, or a Druidic path for example—what virtues are added to this list and why?

Activity 2: Lifestyle—Values and Character in Action

Lifestyle refers to *how* we live our lives. In most circumstances our strongest (most salient) values determine what choices we make in our day-to-day life. When we consider the issue of becoming a leader of a Neopagan tradition, lifestyle takes on more important meaning—that of congruency between the ethics of the faith and the choices of the teacher. Those who will become successful priest/esses are those who manifest the best match between faith and lifestyle. In this fashion, those of you who are seriously considering the ministry or those who are already on this path, taking an honest look at your lifestyle and how it matches up with your religious belief is important. In Neopaganism some of the lifestyle issues include (you may think of this as consistency between what you practice and what you preach):

1. How *green* do you live?—recognizing that the sacredness of the earth is a central tenant of all Neopagan traditions, how you engage in environmentally responsible behavior is a central issue to determine the degree of congruency. This is not to say that issues such as affordability are not considered—rather we look at what we are realistically "capable" of doing and what we are "actually" doing.

2. How do you treat those with less social power in your life or in your community?—recognizing that all Neopagan traditions view divinity in all people, as such looking at how you protect and support those with less is an important source for congruency.

3. How do you treat nonhuman animals?—Neopaganism extends the notion of divinity to nonhuman beings, as such how we engage with, serve, and protect the wild and domestic is an important area to examine.

4. How do you treat your body?—Neopaganism centrally values the body as sacred house of the spirit, just as the earth is the sacred house for the spirit of the Creator/Creatrix; while no one is perfect, this question asks us to consider just how well we take care of our travelling temple. We cannot expect others to respect their bodies if we do not model self-respect and self-love.

5. How do you treat your Self?—Neopaganism centrally values personal growth and the value of each person as having an innate value and message from the Divine. Adherents look toward their priests/esses to determine how they value themselves and how they look for growth and work with imperfections.

6. How do you use language?—what we say carries power, particularly when in a position of authority. Neopaganism values compassion, equality, diversity, and open-mindedness—as such it is absolutely essential for all priests/esses to speak **only** after careful

thought and consideration for any issues of personal bias, stereotyping, exclusionary language, and word choices that diminish another's experience.

Take time to journal about each of these issues as well as brainstorm additional lifestyle areas where you need consistency between what you practice and what you teach.

Conclusion

We may consider Values and Character and Worldview as a triangle. Whereby, each element becomes a central point of focus, but intimately linked to all other points. Our character is the individual expression of how we have come to see the world, our worldview. While our worldview is the living expression of how our values and social groups have interacted and shaped our beliefs about how the world works and our perceptions, how we see the world. Each three points creates the lens behind which our lives and our religious teachings are framed. And as such, self-reflection into how each of these elements works is critical so that we can serve those we work with and the Divine with the openness necessary to heart the Divine's message. Further, crafting the skill of self-reflection is a long step toward reducing challenges associated with values conflicts and ethical dilemmas, all of which will occur as you become more committed toward your spiritual service.

4
The Professional Role

The Occupation of Priest & Priestess

There are two unique ways in which the terms priest and priestess have come to be defined within Neopagan traditions. In the first definition, priest and priestess refer to *any* individual who has dedicated themselves in service to the Goddess and/or God. In this fashion, any individual coming into a Neopagan tradition is a priest/ess of the Divine. Additionally, in traditions that are nonhierarchical in structure all members are priest/priestess and thus seen as having spiritual authority and insight. Within this situation, we find the role of the priest and priestess as an individual who serves the Divine in their day-to-day life and often their private rituals. In this capacity, our focus on manifesting this role is on how we *live* our personal lives in accordance with the tenants and charges of our sense and conception of the Divine. By internalizing the view of ourselves as priest and priestess, we strengthen our personal spiritual identity and our personal commitment to our faith.

The second way priest and priestess is defined is based on tradition. Many Neopagan traditions confer the title of priest and priestess upon an individual when they have completed two year-and-a-day cycles. In this capacity, these titles indicate your commitment to the tradition you are studying and the degree of knowledge you have obtained. Generally, upon the conferring of these titles, you will often be asked to take on a greater leadership role within your tradition's community. This may include teaching or facilitating rituals. However, many individuals may interpret this title similar to the first definition and *not* take on a leadership or professional role. Rather it may remain a confirmation of your spiritual path and commitment to the Goddess and/or God.

In this chapter—and indeed in this text—our focus is on the second definition of the term and specifically in how one becomes a priest/priestess within the context of *service* to other members in the Neopagan community and how this takes on a public and professional leadership role in one's chosen Neopagan tradition and path. As such our chapter is focused on the *professional* and *occupational* elements of what it means to be a Neopagan Priest or Priestess.

Assessing Readiness

The first question all individuals who seek ordination as a priest/ess is to consider whether or not they wish to take on the *professional* responsibilities of that role and in what way they wish to manifest those professional responsibilities. In Neopagan tradition, it is perfectly acceptable to become a priest or priestess and direct your energy toward your own solitary contemplation and private work. Additionally it is equally acceptable to retain this title and choose not to take a leadership role within a coven, group, or grove that you work with. However, if you elect to take on the professional elements of the role, it's important to know your readiness.

Readiness is based on the assessment along five dimensions: spiritual, intellectual, emotional, personal, and professional dimensions.

> **Spiritual readiness** refers to the degree you are committed to your Neopagan beliefs and have a mature, well-integrated understanding of the tenants of your faith. Related to this issue is your own capacity to apply the specific tenants of your traditional/spiritual affiliation in your day-to-day life. Further, do you feel "called" to lead in your tradition? In short, do you feel the best way to manifest your service to the Goddess and/or God is through working directly in service to others in the faith—or is there another path for you to fully manifest your divine purpose?

> **Intellectual readiness** refers to knowledge—do you know *enough* about your faith (including its history, theo/alogies, symbols, ethics and values, cosmologies, and its relationship to wider religious traditions, etc.) and can you articulate what you know in a clear fashion? Does this mean you have to be a genius or a college education? No. What this means is that you demonstrate an expertise in your faith and you demonstrate a capacity to coherently articulate this faith. It also means you have *demonstrated* a successful completion of the educational guidelines specific to your tradition or faith-based affiliation. Remember in the professional role you become the *teacher*—so it is a good idea to have an

image in your mind of your most effective teacher while in school and what it was that made that teacher effective (hopefully they will be a blend of creative, compassionate, and smart).

Emotional readiness refers to your capacity to successfully handle stress and conflict coupled with personal insight and self-reflection into your own emotional challenges. Taking on the *professional* role of priest/ess means you become the emotional touchstone for many of your members; and members will look to you in terms of how to apply the tenants of faith to cope with life's challenges. Additionally, you will also need to be able to negotiate conflicts and threats to your own self esteem as members disagree with you or elect to leave your group—becoming bitter, vengeful or resentful would indicate you might need a new professional role. Further, emotional readiness refers to your capacity to make good on your commitments and express your feelings in assertive, non-aggressive or passive-aggressive ways, expressing a consistent and positive sense of self. Finally, emotional readiness refers to your capacity for insight into your limitations and your talents and your own personal drive for growth. This requires a substantial internal emotional resource and a general capacity for emotional stability.

Personal readiness refers to your capacity to commit to the professional role. If your personal life is chaotic or filled with numerous responsibilities that taking on a leadership role begins to compete with other commitments or relationships, you won't be able to fulfill your duties. If you are in a committed relationship or have children, it's important to talk with your family members to realistically determine how much time you have to devote to members in your Neopagan community. How much time you have to devote to your community is dependent upon how much time you have in your personal life without sacrificing your own down-time or critical family time. Neopagan traditions, unlike other religions, is very flexible and in most instances professional service to the community can successfully occur no more than once a week with some prep time set aside—some only occur during moon cycles or on one of the eight holidays for most traditions.

Professional readiness refers specifically to your skills. Do you have the necessary skills to take on a leadership position? We can assess professional skills in four broad areas: (a) your liturgical/ritualist skills—do you know how to craft and lead rituals and are your rituals situated within the broader theo/alogical constructs of your tradition; (b) counseling skills for pastoral care—do you know how to utilize your faith to help members resolve issues in their personal lives; (c) teaching skills to initiate and mentor other members; and (d) if your work becomes an occupation, you also need to demonstrate administrative and financial readiness—this emerges only if you seek incorporation to become a religious "business" (generally this means seeking tax-exemption under 501(c)(3) IRS code). You will need to have the capacity to manage, operate, maintain and supervise a business environment. It is important to note that not all these professional skill areas may fall into your own goals. For example, and more on this later, some priest/esses focus strictly on a ritualist role. In addition to these four broad areas, some basic skills are required for *all* roles: effective communication, comfort in social situations, and a general capacity to take on a leadership role.

Readiness is often a subject that is uncomfortable for the individual seeking to become a priest/priestess in two ways. First, many individuals have difficulty assessing their skills due to unrealistic self-perception. Unrealistic self-perception may manifest as underestimating your skills due to low self esteem and a lack of confidence or it may manifest as overestimation of your skills. As such it is important to talk with those who know you very well and whom you can receive honest feedback from to discuss your professional goals and readiness. It is additionally important to speak with your "spiritual teachers" to help you evaluate where your strengths are and where growth opportunities occur. It is important to recognize that any readiness areas that need growth does not mean you are not "meant" to be a priest or priestess; rather these allow you to direct your energy toward preparation to ensure your goals manifest. Just remember that assessing your readiness is essential to ensure a positive experience in the role for both you and those you serve.

The Professional Roles

As briefly alluded to in the *professional readiness* definition, the Neopagan Priest/ess can take on three specific professional identities that may or may not co-occur together. These identities are always integrated together when the individual receives the title of High Priest or High Priestess. These three roles are the Ritual Specialist, the Teacher/Mentor, and the Pastoral Counselor. Finally, if you are working in conjunction with a High Priest or High Priestess then you will also be in a position of working to assist them with the day-to-day functioning of the group.

The Professional Role: The Ritual Specialist

Perhaps the most common role that newly ordained priests and priestesses take within their community is that of a ritual specialist. Often beginning prior to ordination, the individual will engage in leading various rituals for the community. For example, in Wicca-based traditions this is often leading Esbats (lunar worship). The ritual specialist is someone who is skilled at creating and facilitating rituals for his or her community. Further the ritual specialist is responsible for maintaining the spiritual calendar for their community—for ensuring that members have consistent opportunities to increase their own experience of the sacred throughout the year.

There are two broad types of rituals that the priest or priestess will be asked to create: a celebration ritual and a task- or work-oriented ritual, which may overlap during holidays. In this fashion, the priest and priestess is required to demonstrate knowledge of:

1. The sacred calendar of the year for their tradition. This includes the recognition that these days are designed to provide adherents with opportunities, not only to come together socially, but to reaffirm their faith, to experience a greater closeness with the divine, and to aid individuals with a sense of security in the unfolding of life—a sacred process that they are a part of and which is larger than any one individual.

2. The lore and symbols associated with each calendar day. The ritual specialist is required to develop rituals that are steeped in the theo/alogical meaning of the day and utilizes the cosmological or mythic lore coupled with symbols that serve to create an atmospheric and emotional environment to support the adherent's sense of mystery and contemplation of the sacred.

3. The steps for successful ritual process. While Neopagan traditions vary somewhat in the specific structure of ritual, all of them follow a general process that includes a welcoming, statement of purpose, casting a circle (thus creating a sacred atmosphere and transforming the mundane environment into a sacred temple), invocation of the divine, blessing and reception of the blessing, closing and disbanding the circle.

4. How to write a ritual that is transformative, as well as fosters participation by members. This means the ritual has a structure that can be readily identified by participants and has easily learned parts for participants to play. At the same time, the ritual does not lose its capacity to impact participants.

5. For work- or task-based rituals (magick, healing, blessings, etc.), the ritual specialist knows how to translate goals into a ritual event—including effectively utilizing symbols that reflect the change the ritual seeks to bring about.

6. Finally, the ritual specialist is very comfortable taking center-stage within the group and demonstrates a capacity to gain and keep the group's attention and keep the group focused on the ritual goals at hand.

There are three primary ways individuals may gain these skills. The first is *in vivo* experience—that is you have attended live and online (online if this is the medium you plan on working) rituals. Through attending rituals you can observe how they are conducted, note what works and what doesn't work from your own personal experience, and gain ideas for creative rituals. Second, reading is critical—the more you know about myth, symbols and ritual structure the more possibilities you have to create effective rituals. Finally, ask for feedback—it can be difficult for the ego, but if you have participants complete an anonymous survey after the ritual to assess what they liked or didn't like about the ritual, you can learn a great deal about where your skills need strengthening and where they are working effectively.

The Professional Role: The Teacher

In many Neopagan traditions, the priest and priestess are utilized to mentor new students and potential initiates. They are often the individuals who provide reading material and oversee competencies of the new members and initiates to learn the beliefs, values, and rituals of the tradition. They are often the primary source of feedback and information about the tradition for new members and initiates. Skills necessary for a Teacher role include:

1. Being able to effectively communicate the tenants of your tradition's beliefs and to be able to orient new members and potential initiates into what is expected of them on the path.

2. Develop a curriculum and specific goals for achievement for the new member or initiate that reflects the necessary skills for a priest or priestess of the tradition.

3. Be able to provide effective teaching strategies to help students learn and to also be able to provide feedback to students to assist them in their spiritual growth.

4. Be able to admit when you don't know something and know how to find the answer. You will have students who come knowing more or come with questions you don't know the answer to. It's okay not to know—just go and read up on it. If a student is reading a text, you don't know but it is related to concepts you want them to learn—read it.

5. Encourage the student to expand the tradition. While it is important for the student to have the foundational knowledge—it is also important for Neopagan traditions that teachers encourage students to extend the knowledge. In the words of Judy Harrow: "Nobody can impose uniformity of belief or practice upon us, and may all the Gods forbid that anyone ever could!"[1]. This doesn't mean all ideas are a go—sometimes a student's ideas and interpretations just aren't compatible with the tradition. Under these circumstances, it's important to be honest with the student and suggest alternatives for their faith expression. Sometimes a tradition simply isn't the right fit. However, if the student's ideas extend the tradition's own theo/alogy they should be encouraged. The goal of the teacher is to prepare the student for their own future leadership—we can do this through encouraging them to risk for a deeper theo/alogical understanding.

Gaining skills to prepare for this role is two-fold. First, you need to have a solid intellectual and spiritual understanding of the parameters of your tradition and of the broader encompassing faith (for example, if you are a "Green Witch" you also understand Wicca in general; if you are a "Dianic Witch", you also understand Wicca in general; if you are a Druid, you understand the broader Neopagan field). Knowing the specifics and the generalities will allow you to see the direction your student is moving in and to determine if their ideas extend your tradition's depth. To gain a robust intellectual understanding it's important to read, read, and read; if you can attend workshops and festivals and online groups, great, that allows you to engage with other traditions and swap ideas.

Also many individuals have *multiple* initiations or educational experiences within diverse traditions before settling on one core belief. It's very good to explore diverse paths and educational opportunities as each of these will serve to help you communicate and teach your students. Multiple commitments should never be seen as a "bad thing"—it reflects the process of spiritual identity formation and growth and can be a well for tradition development.

Finally, the next method of teacher-preparation is knowing how you come to understand the processes of teaching and learning. We've all had some encounter with the educational system and with the role of the teacher. Chances are also high that you've come to realize there are lots of different methods of teaching and you've also experienced poor teaching. Poor teaching occurs in two fashions: the failure of the teacher to adapt to the learning needs of the student or a lack of knowledge in how to teach. Poor learning occurs in two ways: failure of the teacher to adapt the material in a way that works best for the student's innate learning skills or a lack of motivation on the part of the student.

To avoid the pitfalls of the one-size fits all teaching method, it's important to know how your student learns. Most individuals know how they learn best. If you asked yourself how you learn best, chances are you'll have a rather clear idea. While you won't be able to adapt all material to suit each student's need—indeed this may not be possible in large learning environments—you can explore some alterations: such as self-study and reducing time constraints for students; incorporating audio or visual methods for learning; emphasizing hands-on learning over private study; establishing small discussion group study; etc. If you are looking to improve motivation, the first thing to assess is success. How successful has the student been thus far? Sometimes we need to adjust the requirements and break them down into smaller, more readily achievable parts to provide earlier feelings of success and competency. This can go a long way to improving learning.

The Professional Role: The Pastoral Counselor

The final role that the priest and priestess might take on is the pastoral counselor. This is a complex role that generally requires a greater emotional intimacy with your members. In this role, you're responsibilities often include counseling, attending to the "sick-bed", working with families facing or having faced a death, and spiritual mentoring (a deepening of the student's intellectual skills seen in the teaching role). This is a complex role that not only requires a substantial amount of knowledge in your faith, but also requires the additional skills:

- being able to *apply* theo/alogical frameworks to address a member's personal situations—thus helping members look to resolving situations through the supportive framework of their faith.

- Having *pastoral* counseling skills (effective listening, effective problem-solving, grief and crisis counseling, etc) and knowing when to refer members to professional psychological help.

- Skills for spiritual mentoring—strategies to facilitate members to deepen their faith and sense of the sacred.

Building pastor counseling skills often requires substantial training in the theo/alogy of your tradition and training associated with psychotherapy. In most hierarchically structured Neopagan groups, the priest and priestess will generally deploy these skills in support of the High Priest or Priestess (or Elder) when they are unable to meet these goals. Nevertheless, pastoral skills are essential for the priest or priestess who plans on having a more involved and intimate relationship with their members. Given the depth necessary to address this role, we'll be looking at it more fully in the next chapter and throughout the remainder of the text.

The Practical Boundaries of the Role

All professional roles have boundaries or limits—the role of the priest or priestess is no different. There are two ways in which this role is limited. The first is when the priest or priestess occurs within a hierarchically organized structure—whereby there is an elder or High Priest/ess supervising one's work. When the priest/ess occurs within the context of an organized clergy structure in Neopaganism, they generally work as an assistant to the Elder of the structure (when there is none, they are ultimately in charge and the issues addressed in this text can be readily applied to an Elder or High Priest/ess). This means they deploy their skills and roles in ways that are defined by the structure. The second is the parameters of law and ethics. As such, it is important to know how your tradition defines the boundaries of your role and its responsibilities.

When we examine the role within the context of the law we encounter a few important issues. First, religion is a constitutionally guaranteed right—you can practice any faith you wish and you can call yourself by any title within that faith. However, where the law becomes important is when your organization seeks 501(c)(3)[2] status—this is a tax exemption status. Contrary to popular belief you do not need this status to be a recognized faith or congregation. This only allows you to accept financial support that is tax exempt. This means you as a priest or priestess can be paid, within reason, for your role. However, tax exemption status means that you cannot, under any circumstance, engage in any type of organizing political action. This can be a challenge for the Neopagan as many Neopagan groups are political and socially motivated to strive for social and environmental justice. Thus if you use your position as priest or priestess to expound on a political situation, you could face legal challenges and fines.

Each state does have unique requirements in terms of performing marriages and civil unions. Priest and priestesses who engage in these rites *must* ensure that their religious credentialing and affiliation is recognized by the state *before* they engage in these types of ceremonies.

A word on counseling: in general all states have passed laws to prohibit non-licensed professionals from counseling. It is thus illegal to advertize oneself as a psychologist or mental health counselor without a license *unless* you are working under direct supervision of a licensed professional. Licensing often requires at least two years attendance to an *accredited* Master's program in counseling or clinical social work—this is the *minimum* requirement. However, pastoral counseling is often a non-licensed form of counseling due to its religious association—but individuals *must* know the parameters of counseling. As a pastoral counselor you are **not** permitted to diagnose or advertise that you **treat** specific psychological disorders (or diseases for that matter). If you encounter a member who is manifesting profound personal or psychological distress, refer your member to a licensed counseling professional. It is a good idea to network with area counselors to find those who are open to Neopagan patients. They will generally be very open to working with you in the care of your members.

Also, states have unique laws regarding privileged communication for communication that occurs within the context of a discussion between priest/ess and member. While law often protects religious communication, these situations raise an important ethical issue of not only protecting the member, but the community. In general, it is very important that you know your states laws on what types of communication must be reported by law to authorities. While it can be important to establish confidentiality between you and your members, some situations (for example by not reporting child abuse, threats of harm to others, or elder abuse) when not reported raise a question of your faith and your ethics and may also result in legal action against you.

A word on healing—many Neopagan priests and priestess also incorporate healing modalities within their community. It is illegal within the United States to make any claim of treating a specific disease or disorder without a valid medical license. Further, while individuals are permitted to utilize and seek religious-based healing methods, it is very important to know how well you are protected should the individual have a negative outcome from either the healing modality utilized or if they should refuse treatment by a licensed physician. It is not uncommon for a religious leader to be held responsible in the event of death or injury of an individual who rejected medical interventions due to their membership within the specific religious environment.

Professional Development

When we've achieved the title of priest or priestess, we have something to celebrate. Yet, we must also recognize that this is not an endpoint. When we deploy this title as a professional role, we are being charged with the responsibility of continued growth. In this fashion, we are being asked to consider what do we know and what do we still need to know? New members and initiates have access to such a wide range of material and diverse experiences—many even hold titles from other traditions and thus agree to become a student within another—as such it is important to recognize that as a priest or priestess you must have a means of continued development to ensure you meet the needs of your students and can contribute something *new* to their experiences. Second, Neopaganism values the role of continued learning. Thus as we engage in continued professional development we are not only fulfilling our role to our students and initiates, but we are also meeting an underlying ethic of our faith—we are *living* our faith.

What constitutes professional development? Training in other traditions, attending a seminary either focused to your faith or another faith, attending workshops and community festivals, joining an online community, and reading. Reading is perhaps the one aspect of professional development that is accessible at all times and allows us to focus our skill development to areas where we need more help. Additionally, consider obtaining a subscription to several leading Neopagan publications such as *SageWoman, Beltane Papers,* or *Pomegranate* to keep you up-to-date on current trends, contemporary issues impacting the Neopagan community, and theological developments. Attending workshops and community events helps you extend your network of contacts and resources for information that may arise in a professional situation (and always get contact information and note where and when you met the individual). Further if you attend workshops, training sessions, a seminary school, or achieve ordination in another tradition—these all become added to your *curriculum vitae* (your professional resume). If you attend a seminary or a more formalized training, note your courses you've taken on this resume. And having this resume available to students and new members is a great way for them to gain confidence in your skills.

※

However you ultimately opt to express your professional role, the key to remember is this: know yourself, know your path, know your students, and know the law. If you do this, there's a good chance you'll do just fine in your professional role. You'll be able to make adjustments to your work so that you remain consistent and in concert with your professional obligations. You'll approach students with a high-degree of professionalism and thus, not only encourage them to remain in the tradition, but also communicate confidence and trust. And finally, knowing your professional boundaries and sticking to them, you'll also model to your students and the community both within and without your tradition an positive image.

5
The Pastoral Relationship

Defining the Pastoral Role

In the previous chapter, we discussed three broad roles that the priest and priestess may play within their community. In this chapter we'll be unpacking the most complex role that the priest or priestess may play in their community, that of the "Pastor". Pastor is literally defined as an individual who has "spiritual" care of his or her religious community. Pastors are the men and women who become the spiritual resources for their communities when challenges strike in order to facilitate members in the meaning-making process, resiliency and successful coping. Pastors are those members of their religious community who are capable of bringing a theological understanding to everyday experiences and help their members learn to *live* a spiritually infused life. The Neopagan pastor is able to utilize the myths and symbols of their traditional beliefs to facilitate each member's capacity to see the Divine in their day-to-day experiences.

The role of the Neopagan Pastor involves three skill areas merged together: mentor, pedagogical expert, and counselor. Within the role of spiritual mentor, the pastor is able to facilitate spiritual growth of each member of the community. As an expert in pedagogy, the pastor is able to *teach* the necessary religious skills required for each member to initiate into their tradition and to become full participants within its ritual life. And finally, as a counselor, the pastor is able to provide supportive counseling interventions to help members in their community cope with life stressors; further the pastor is able to frame counseling interventions within the theological context. Over the next few pages, we'll explore each of these roles in-depth.

Before moving further, it is important to note of all the roles a priest or priestess may play, the most daunting and skilled is that of the pastor. Not every individual seeking the priest/priestesshood or even advanced degrees will necessarily make a good pastor. At the conclusion of this chapter, we'll look at the issue of readiness to better help you determine whether or not pursuing this element of the profession is where your calling is. Further, due to the nature of the role merging complex skills, I generally recommend that full embrace of this role occur *after* the you have achieved an elder status of High Priest/ess or hold a doctorate in ministry (D.Min) or have graduate background in counselor, social work, or psychology (minimum of a Master's degree). All of which would sufficiently prepare you to take on the full scope and function of this role with little difficulty. Given the educational and experience requirements of this role, this chapter will look introduce you to the parameters of the practice. It will also provide an introduction to the basic techniques of each role element and provide you with ideas for further education.

The Spiritual Mentor

The spiritual mentor is an expert in how individuals develop their religious and spiritual identities and come to commit themselves to a faith or even break away from that faith. Because the mentor understands the stages of religious development that individuals move through and how their internal view of their religion influences this development, the mentor is able to foster that individual's spiritual growth. In other words the Neopagan mentor knows:

(a) how and why people come to the Neopagan path, particularly the tradition they are working in;
(b) how individuals grow along this path; and
(c) how to mentor (facilitate) their growth on this path.

In order to understand this role it's important to understand a few things about how we formulate our religious identity. Identity, as a broad concept, refers to our understanding of who we are and how we would define ourselves, coupled with our group associations and our positions within those groups. Generally how we feel about ourselves is deeply linked to our relationships with our larger social networks—either in conflict (whereby we see ourselves one way and a group defines us differently) or in congruency (there is a high-degree of match between how we perceive ourselves and how others do). Our identity is always changing as our relationships to the world around us change and the roles we play in groups change (known as social identities or role identities). Our religious affiliation forms one element of our identity known as *religious identity*. The degree of saliency (personal importance) of this identity depends on the degree of our connection and commitment to this affiliation. One's religious identity is often a cornerstone in how an individual "sees" themselves in relation to and organizes their behavior toward the world around them.

Peek[1] has suggested that we develop our religious identity through three stages: (a) Ascribed identity; (b) Chosen identity; and (c) Declared identity. When we hold an *ascribed* religious identity it refers to our religious identity as one that is given to us by our parents and cultural tradition we are born into. Since Neopaganism is a new religion, we are only now just beginning to see children being ascribed the Neopagan faith from their families. Generally during this stage, the child or adolescent typically does not reflect on the actual personal meaning of their faith, but sees it as an element of their relationship to their family. During this stage, the spiritual mentoring needs are focused toward developmentally appropriate education, while at the same time working holistically with the family and providing skills to family members to support the spiritual growth and exploration of their children. Because Neopaganism values freedom and choice, the Neopagan spiritual mentor encourages and supports families to allow their children to not only develop a sense of security and acceptance within the Neopagan community but the opportunity to explore their own calling.

During the *chosen identity* stage (generally the earliest time for this to begin is mid-adolescence), the individual begins to consciously and actively choose their religious identity and begin to develop a sense of personal meaning. In the choosing stage, the individual seeks information, reflects on what they know and what they don't know, and begins to expand their knowledge of the social and behavioral (ritual) requirements of their faith. They may experiment with greater incorporation of religious behavior in their day-to-day life and they may become increasingly more concerned with answering larger questions of life (meaning-making, afterlife, and purpose). During this stage, the individual begins to see him/herself personally relating to their chosen religion—they do not see themselves as relating to the faith because *another* individual told them to or required it[2]. The spiritual mentoring goals of this stage are to provide ample opportunities for each individual to expand their knowledge and understanding depths of their faith. Within the Neopagan context, this would include exploring how the individual came to their path, their expectations and goals, strategies for deepening their sense of the Divine in their everyday life, providing reading recommendations, discussing fears and sources of anxiety, discussing issues of social acceptance and support, and spiritual activities to strengthen the individual's sense of self as a Neopagan.

In the final stage, the individual has developed a mature and reflected religious identity. The identity has become a *public* identity. The individual experiences a sense of certainty in their choice and will seek opportunities to assert and express their identity. The individual has gained a substantial understanding of their faith and its tenets and readily applies them in their day-to-day life. Individuals in this stage also look toward how they may become positive ambassadors for their faith. In religions marked by prejudice and misunderstanding, during this stage, members often seek to reeducate the public toward tolerance, acceptance, and the recognition of the positive and affirming elements of their path. The spiritual mentor in this stage often focuses their guidance toward helping the individual choose their religious direction, including opting for the priest/priesthood or taking on greater responsibility within the community. The mentor may also help the individual explore ways to positively assert their identity in the larger community or to provide support for the individual to cope with prejudice. The mentor may provide more complex exercises to help further the individual's sense of connection with the Divine and will generally rely on more in-depth theo/alogical conceptions to foster growth and the merging of the individual's religious identity to their everyday identity. The spiritual mentor in this role may also help act as a counsel to a clergy member who may be experiencing doubt, disappointment with themselves and their capacity to live their faith, or who may be faced with a tough decision where another community member is concerned and simply needs a sounding board on the theo/alogical and spiritual aspects of their conflicts.

While this three-stage model is beneficial for the spiritual mentor, the Neopagan mentor faces some unique differences from say a Jewish or Christian or Islamic mentor. Most Neopagans come to Neopaganism following a break from their religion of origin. This often comes with two specific challenges: first, their break from their religion-of-origin may have occurred due to a crisis and an emotional loss/betrayal of faith and/or the shift into Neopaganism may also risk the loss of intimate connections with families or community members one's prior religious identity facilitated. Because many Neopagans come to the diverse traditions following a *break* with a tradition of origin, *ascribed stage* makes little sense for a majority of Neopagans' religious development. Rather, this first stage may best replaced by another stage I call the *Dispersal,* meaning the individual coming to Neopaganism seeks to disperse the energy and commitments of their previous religious affiliations in favor of a new path.

Individuals may come to this stage even after completing all three stages within another religion, just as individuals entering Neopaganism may in turn disperse Neopaganism in favor of a different identity. During this stage, the spiritual mentor should explore with the individual the circumstances that led to their leaving the previous religious identity (and that includes identities such as atheist and agnostic). They should also explore with the individual what they have gained *and* lost in their leaving—particularly as some losses may prove over time so powerful that the individual leaves Neopaganism to return and recommitment to their tradition of origin. For example, for some individuals the loss of their parental relationships over religion can lead to that individual returning back to their "ascribed" identity to repair these relationships. It is not the spiritual mentor's place to position their mentee for any decision, rather the spiritual mentor is there to serve the individual to help them articulate their decisions and firm up what is most important to them and will bring about the greatest benefits. If the mentee clearly demonstrates a desire to move toward a Neopagan path, then the spiritual mentor can provide this individual with a spiritual and ritual exercise to symbolize the dispersing of the old religious energy to welcome in the new. The mentor can also help the individual assimilate what positives they have gained of their prior faith commitments to help them develop a cohesive and mature religious identity and one that does not foster resentment, hate, or prejudice toward another faith. Further still, the Neopagan mentor may also find their mentee really needs to return to their faith-of-origin and should have strong knowledge of other faiths to be able to facilitate this individuals healing and return.

Another popular perspective of how individuals grow in their religious commitments that specifically relates to how individuals leave one faith for another is Rambo's 1993 **Theory of Religious Conversion**[3]. Conversion[4] is the religious term utilized to describe how one individual comes to identify themselves with a *new* religion or fundamentally new belief about the nature of reality and the Divine and their relationship to these concepts. Research into the process of conversion has shown that there are two ways in which individuals come to this point: collective social pressure (significant others are doing it) or a charismatic and persuasive leader. For example on October 14, 1956, a Hindu "untouchable[5]" BR Ambedkar led two million other untouchables to convert to Buddhism in a single day. While not common, we do know that such events generally follow social principals of a charismatic leader who is able to provide a meaningful solution for his or her followers to undo or change a particularly painful circumstance in their lives. In this case to redirect their faith to a religion that would not dislocate them from society. However, most conversions are small scale and individual in nature. Rambo defines the process of conversion as developing across seven stages: (a) context, (b) crisis, (c) quest, (d) encounter, (e) interaction, (f) commitment, and (g) consequences. These states can overlap or recur many times in an individual's life as they "change" their religious identity or reaffirm it.

Context
Stage Definition
Context refers to the social factors that surround the individual's life who is seeking conversion. It includes their family and social contexts,

as well as their own internal processes and value systems. It is the "stuff" that all individuals transitioning to a new religion will bring with them, not only in the process of the transition, but also throughout their time committed to the new religion. These outer social contexts will serve to facilitate or inhibit to varying degrees the conversion process. For example, individuals converting to a majority religion that is widely accepted will be more likely to find wider social support than those who are converting to a lesser known or minority religion. And depending on how the individual views their religious change as a salient social identity over other social identities, social approval may influence the degree to which they commit to a new religion.

Context Mentoring Tips

This is a time of assessing and asking the individual to reflect on their lives and what factors have shaped them, both related to their religious identity and also to their outlook of life as a whole. What values do they hold and where have these come from? During this time it is important to create a safe environment to allow for the expression of the individual's total religious experience. It is also important to encourage individuals converting throughout their process to continue reflecting and to facilitate them in integrating their prior religious experiences into a cohesive story/narrative of their religious identity. Additionally, the spiritual mentor should look at how they craft the context to support and encourage the individual's successful transition.

Crisis
Stage Definition

Religious crisis often reflects an internal sense of dis-ease for one's current faith and its capacity to answer growing theological questions. This crisis may be felt as a painful change or it may occur subtly over years as the individual encounters more and more theological concepts and symbols that do not match their own sense of the Divine. For many Neopagans, crisis often occurs from a growing sense of mismatch between their religion of origin and their sense of truth about how the world works. It may be brought about by negative experiences within their religion or simply through a growing dis-ease with faiths that do not necessarily focus on the Earth as a central spiritual figure. Many Neopagans report coming to the faith because of a growing need for new models of the Divine that embrace an inclusive picture of Male and Female, Animal and Human, Earth and the Ephemeral.

Crisis Mentoring Tips
If you encounter a mentee in this stage, as with all types of Crises, this is a time for being calm and allowing the individual to fully articulate what it is about their situation they wish to change. Sometimes they ultimately wish to stay within their faith and change it from the inside. A wonderful example of this can be found in Carol Christ and her colleague Judith Plaskow. Both are feminist theologians who felt that their faiths of origin (Christianity in the former and Judaism in the latter) were not sufficient for them due to their lack of a Divine Feminine figure that they felt was spiritually fulfilling and necessary for a rich religious life. Carol Christ left the Church and pursued the Neopagan path of the Goddess tradition. In contrast, Plaskow remained a Jew but has worked actively to redefine Jewish rituals and theological concepts to reawaken its dormant appreciation for women and the Divine woman. The spiritual mentor's job at this time is to help individuals really flesh out what changes they would like to make and see happen and what are the best ways to do it. It requires that the mentor know the parameters of their tradition and what it can offer and to be honest and authentic with the individual if it is not the best fit.

Quest
Stage Definition
Once a crisis has occurred that has led the individual to feel their current faith as it stands is no longer where they wish to be, they must begin a journey to find the faith that does resonate. This new faith will often provide them with new ideas and strategies to cope with their life challenges. During this stage, the individual often explores a wide range of options. They may be reading material and engaging in Internet searchers. Within the Neopagan context, individuals may begin to attend open rituals or festivals or join an online discussion group. In most cases individuals are looking for that flash of intuition or that "ah-hah" moment where they find that combination of beliefs, concepts, and values that most resonate with where they are now and where they would like to see their faith transition toward.

Quest Mentoring Tips
If you have a formal encounter with a mentee during this stage, it is important that the spiritual mentor be a resource for information. Further, at this stage, the mentor can help the individual clarify their beliefs

and what they feel they need. Often times, our religious needs during a transition are vague or only feelings. We have a sense that "something" else is out there, but we don't know what it is. Through open-ended questioning and journal activities, the spiritual mentor can help individuals come to a greater understanding of what changes they are specifically seeking and help guide the individual toward a path with a good fit.

Encounter
Stage Definition
This is the moment where the seeker becomes more intimately engaged with the new faith they have chosen. There are two issues that emerge in this stage; the first is the actual quality or tone of the mentor–mentee relationship that will develop. As this is the first formal interaction between the seeker and their new faith, the tone set during this period of time can go a long way to shaping the degree to which the individual will relate to the new faith. Also at this time, the spotlight is on how the faith defines how an individual can transition to that faith, including what changes in the seeker's current beliefs or social circumstances are needed for the change. In Neopaganism, there is traditionally a wider acceptance of past experiences and no demands on relinquishing one's prior beliefs; however traditions do vary. Finally during this period, the mentee will have an opportunity to explore what benefits the new faith will bring to them.

Encounter Mentoring Tips
The mentor sets the tone for their faith and how well the seeker will engage with it. During this encounter the mentor must be able to provide a clear description of their tradition and also allow for the seeker to ask numerous questions. The spiritual mentor in this stage should encourage the mentee to ask as many questions as they need and remind them to ask any questions in the future. If this is the *first* time you've encountered this individual, than the activities of the previous stages are important to work with. Also during this time it is absolutely critical that you know your tradition's parameters for conversion: What does the individual need to know and do in order to successfully transition into the new faith.

Interaction
Stage Definition
This is also known as the "encapsulation" stage. During this stage, the spiritual mentor creates a safe holding environment for the mentee that allows them to fully experience and immerse themselves in the new faith. In unhealthy traditions, this stage often corresponds to pathological religious indoctrination—whereby the individual may be literally cut-off from other environments that might counter their new beliefs. During this stage there are four primary interactions that emerge to facilitate the transition to the new faith:

> (a) relationships, which create and consolidate emotional bonds to the group; (b) rituals, which provide, through the repetition of physical actions, "embodied or holistic knowledge" as opposed to mere cognitive understanding; (c) rhetoric, which includes new uses of language, new metaphors that serve as "a vehicle for the transformation of consciousness," and new narratives that provide a reframed perspective of the self and the self's place in the larger scheme of things; as well as (d) roles, which provide new expectations of behaviors consonant with the potential convert's ascribed status within the group.[6]

I also consider this as the "deepening" stage, whereby the individual immerses themselves within the new faith and explores how it relates to their own personal life.

Interaction Mentoring Tips
The spiritual mentor during this stage focuses on building a more intimate relationship as well as provides opportunities for the individual to become more deeply engaged with the larger group. During this stage, the mentor should assist the individual in learning the parameters of ritual participation, particularly if the individual has little to no prior related experience with Neopagan rituals. Further the mentor should begin to focus discussions on the broader symbols and myths of the tradition (for example in Wicca, this might include looking at the triple Goddess and discussing its personal meaning for the individual). This is the time of providing activities to the mentee to deepen their personal understanding of their new faith and how it manifests in their life. Also at this time, the spiritual mentor will discuss the process of initiation and education within the tradition.

Commitment
Stage Definition
During this stage the seeker has become committed to the new religion. In most Neopagan traditions this emerges as initiation. This is the moment when the individual often takes on greater responsibility within the tradition and may also help in mentoring other students. In most religions, this would be the point where the individual's commitment is honored ceremonially/ritualistically within a public setting with the wider religious community to bear witness to and thus socially confirm the individual's new religious identity.

Commitment Mentoring Tips
During this stage, the spiritual mentor should have been providing a range of support and encouragement for the individual throughout their initiation period, culminating in their ceremony. Discussions and spiritual activities should be focused on what it means to be committed to the faith/tradition and what responsibilities, not just benefits, come with this commitment. This is the stage where the mentor helps the mentee reexamine their decision to ensure that it is the right one for them at this point in life. The mentor may help the individual develop a new narrative that reflects their new religious identity as defined by this faith. This may emerge as an activity of reflection on where they have been and where they are now and how they have grown. Commitment in Neopagan traditions are often reinforced through the use of structured lessons (discussed shortly), whereby individuals gain a sense of movement and success throughout their work. If they have an opportunity to discuss their "homework" with their mentor, this can give them greater access to meaning and a more confident and deeper transitioned religious identity. Initiation is often a very emotional time, both of nervousness and excitement and the mentor should encourage their mentee to discuss all their fears and excitements.

Consequence
Stage Definition
This is the final stage of conversion, which often lasts for years following the initial initiation/commitment to the new faith. The term "consequence" refers to the outcomes of the change, which may be positive or negative depending on the overall experience the individual has or had in the faith. We may see this is a stage unfold in elders of a tradition or in those who transition out of a tradition. In both situa-

tions, individuals engage in self-reflection (ideally) about where they are and what has or has not occurred in their lives based on their religious choices and expectations.

Consequence Mentoring Tips
Most mentors are mentoring other mentors at this moment. It can be a good time to have a group of just mentors and elders in a tradition to discuss openly and freely their own experiences in their conversion and how they have changed and grown. Including sources of frustration and remaining religious questions. This can be a great time to re-examine one's religious choice to ensure it remains vital and fresh, rather than "going through the motions". When this occurs in an individual who is leaving the group, the mentor should take the time to allow the individual to express their need for change, their anxieties about changing, and to even provide a ritual to allow them to make a clean break from their group.

The final model of value to understanding religious development within the context of mentoring is James Fowler's **Faith Developmental Theory**[7]. This model remains a cornerstone of all pastoral education courses and religious education in general. Fowler based his model on prior stage-development theories emerging from psychology such as Piaget's theory of cognitive development in children and Kohlberg's theory of moral development, as well as Eriksons's life cycle theory[8]. It is important to note that developmental stage theories, which posit all individuals must successfully move through the prior stage and that growth moves in an upward fashion, have garnered a great deal of contemporary criticism in that they often fail to recognize that most of us move in and out of stages and move laterally rather than hierarchically. The only exception of to this process is cognitive development whereby skills depend on biological availability (although this too is not fixed and immutable). Further, many stage theories emerge from within the context of White, Christian and often male backgrounds and may fail to fully capture the wider ways in which all individuals may grow in their identity development, their faith, and their moral development. In this fashion, when we explore Fowler's view, it's important to keep these constraints in mind.

Finally one last note about Fowler's view: the model assumes religious development begins in childhood and moves upwards to adulthood in an appropriate fashion whereby individuals who do not successfully transition from a prior developmental stage to the next reflect religious immaturity. There is no room for religious exploration and self-*redefinition*. As you read through the definitions, chances are you'll find that these stages repeat or are absent depending on your own religious development and transitions—thus the ages can only be understood in approximate terms. Further there is a distinct value judgment in terms of what reflects the ideal religious expression. In this fashion, I personally, find this model problematic given the sheer plurality of religious expression seen in our world and the myriad of ways in which individuals redefine their religious selves. As such throughout the descriptions, you will find the original Fowler definition followed by my modifications to reflect a more unbiased vision that is lateral rather than hierarchical—whereby each stage is privileged for offering a valid and unique vision of faith.

Intuitive–Projective Faith
Stage Definition
Approximate age 3–7

This is a fantasy-filled stage where the child is beginning to integrate the world as a whole into their self-perceptions. It is a stage where the child begins to comprehend death, birth, and even sexuality (although often not with full consciousness). During this stage, the child becomes integrated into their family's religious tradition. The term projective is the child's general ego-centric focus, where they come to understand the world by imposing (projecting) their personal experience on to it (*the world functions as I feel or based on what I need*), rather than how others tell them they "should" experience it. During this stage, it is the child's questioning of the world around them and their own processing that dominates—often to the frustration of their parents.

Revision Point: we may also see this stage as one that could actually define a faith itself. Individuals who never subscribe to a specific religious orientation but imagine and create their own syncretic (merging multiple religious together or religious themes and ideas) view, may remain in this creative and imagined religious life. Unlike children, they would manifest depth in their narratives (what stories they tell about their faith and themselves, how they "talk" about their faith), intuition, and creative inspiration. This may be best understood as a *subjective–constructionist* faith—whereby faith is emergent based solely on one's intuitive understanding of the universe and how they integrate many stories and impressions of the world around them into a cohesive whole.

IP Mentoring Tips
While children are not common in Neopaganism, there is a growing

body of children born into these paths. As such, some degree of mentoring becomes necessary (more on this in our chapter on children) for children. Children can master basic theological concepts through storytelling and hands-on learning methods. Children can be vibrant sources for engagement and can be highly creative. However, it is important to note that children can become anxious and fearful if exposed to too many distressing theological stories. This is unlikely within Neopagan traditions which do not foster concepts of sin and evil. The mentor with children at this age should be enthusiastic, creative, and energetic and structure their spiritual methods for illustrating a key concept over short durations of time. Finally, a fun activity is to have the children to create their own stories, which in Neopagan traditions encourages the maintenance of creativity and its privileging in these paths whereby individuals co-create meaning over time.

For the adult coming to a Neopagan tradition with a syncretic or *subjective–constructionist* faith identity some key points the mentor should be aware of. First, the individual is making a decision to commit to a path that they have little to no immediate control of in shaping. This could indicate a really potent shift for this individual to relinquish a certain degree of power and authority and the mentor should explore this and help the individual adjust. Optionally, the individual may exhibit a greater mismatch with or a resistance to a Neopagan tradition that is more rigid in power structures and new members are seen in clear subordinate positions. The mentor should be aware of this *before* the individual is placed in a psychologically and spiritually untenable position. Thus an individual who has gone it alone with their own ideas should be allowed to articulate what has changed in their spiritual conceptions that they are joining a group with a clear theological vision and how do they feel about this.

You may also find yourself in a position to mentor someone who is a "solitary" practitioner and may be creating their own faith—in this fashion the primary goal is to help them develop meaning and coherency in their imaginal processes so that what they create is fulfilling to them. Encouraging them to express their creativity and own storytelling and myth-making capacity is ideal here.

Mythic–Literal Faith
Stage Definition
During this stage, the child (>7 and pre-adolescence) begins to incorpo-

rate the beliefs and stories of their family's religion. They are better able to perspective-take and thus the meaning others attribute to religion become more important. During this stage, faith is often interpreted literally and concretely. Children are able to describe their faith in specific terms often highlighting key rituals and stories that define it. This is not a reflective stage, but often fulfills a social role, rather than a "spiritual" one.

Revision Point: Some religious traditions may be manifested as this stage. When they are dominated by this stage, they often have sacred texts and stories that are interpreted as "literal" and historical facts. In this capacity the religious emphasis becomes modeling oneself after actions of those depicted in texts and where moral authority is privileged to sacred texts, which are seen as actual words of god. Many Islamic and Christian traditions are steeped in this faith-based stage. Myths are viewed as literal, historical events; rather than symbolic or mystical tools for deepening one's relationship.

ML Mentoring Tips

If you are mentoring a young person in this stage, they are highly receptive to learning and incorporating the traditions of the faith. This is not a reflective time (although I would argue that you can always engage in reflection with children providing it is developmentally appropriate). Activities are designed to continue teaching the myths and symbols of the faith and how these illustrate deeper theological concepts. In this fashion, the goal is no longer story telling alone, but rather to use stories as a means to foster discussion on the underlying concepts of your theological tradition. Both this stage and the previous have a great deal of overlap with the pedagogical elements of the pastor's role.

Neopaganism in general does not foster literal thinking, but rather sees myth as the means of deepening one's aspect with the divine. If you are working with an adult who is very concrete or has just come to Neopaganism from a concrete faith, then the mentoring should be focused on deepening their understanding of myth—how it relates to them, what concepts of life does myth illustrate, what are the moral or spiritual implications of the story. Creative-based activities may also help the individual engage in more symbolic analysis as can asking questions to facilitate deeper engagement with the text.

Synthetic–Conventional Faith
Stage Definition
Emerging in Adolescence.

During this stage of faith development, faith serves a social function and becomes increasingly incorporated into identity. Adolescents seeking to break from tradition and to clarify their own individual sense of self may break from family-of-origin religions at this time. Individuals with a high need for social acceptance may remain in the family's religion to ensure social acceptance (particularly if the religion is one that is in the majority *and* provides meaningful peer interactions or is the dominant religion within that individual's community context). During this stage the adolescent has begun to develop and internalize the values and beliefs of their faith if they have retained it.

Revised Point: Religions where the emphasis is on community and social identity are often linked to this stage. For example Judaism is *both* a religion and a community/cultural identity that are inseparable. In this capacity embracing one's full Jewishness means to not only internalize the beliefs and values and traditions of the religion, but to also be embraced by a community's ethnic identity. In these instances, the religion serves the community and the individual within the community to keep cohesiveness and unity.

SC Mentoring Tips
The spiritual mentor may encounter the adolescent under two circumstances. The first and less common is the teen is the child of another member in the group OR, and more common, the teen is seeking to explore alternative faith-based options away from their family. The mentor in the latter position must come to a few decisions (again discussed later in this text), but if opting to work with the adolescent, then the goal is providing information and guidance, as well as pacing. Adolescents are still testing their identities and thus mentors need to be flexible and recognize change as a part of normal development. Additionally, the adolescent experiences their choices with fervor and emotion that can, and does, wane depending on their social/peer needs and their growth. So as a mentor, the goal is to allow the adolescent room to explore but not have to commit.

In an adult mentee, this period may be that they are breaking form one religion and moving into the Neopagan tradition and their goal is to seek a new spiritual path *and* a strong community to interact with. The mentor should facilitate this social linkage and aid the individual in acquiring the necessary "social" and "spiritual" skills to help them relate. Also during this stage the mentee may need concrete information about beliefs and values clarification to help them transition to a new community.

Individuative–Reflective Faith
Stage Definition
Young Adulthood.

This is the time when individuals move away from spiritual beliefs as defined by the group and seek their own deepening of their beliefs. They begin to explore their understanding of the world around them, the nature of the Divine, and often begin to take a critical look at the faith they are involved with to assess whether it is still resonating. This is the questioning stage ("quest" in Rambo). During this stage the individual will either come to a deeper recommitment to their faith of origin or change altogether.

Revised Point: We also see this stage where the emphasis is on reflection and personal meaning-making manifested in many religions. For example, we may find this in several Neopagan traditions where the goal is focused toward self-development only. Many westernized Buddhist traditions emphasize deep inner reflection to break free from confining or unhealthy patterns in thought, emotion, and behavior. And we also see the emphasis on self-development and growth in New Age spiritualities.

IR Mentoring Tips
When you are working with a mentee in this stage, chances are this corresponds to their first encounter with your Neopagan group. They are looking at joining and are testing the waters to see if the beliefs of your tradition match their growing awareness of the changes they are seeking and wish to make (and with Neopaganism this is not necessarily confined to young adulthood, as many Neopagans come to the faith in their mid-life). This is a time of providing activities that promote clarification of their goals and beliefs, deepening awareness of the Divine as it is explained in your tradition, in their lives; and exploring what the individual will likely gain by their transition. If they have grown up in the faith, this is often the time they will seek initiation and thus need assistance on examining their commitment and their reasons for committing to the faith. This may also be a reactive stage, where an individual's own deepening thought leads them to resist or react against the faith they are

engaged with—individuals may not feel confident or certain that leaving is what they want, but may test the boundaries and their own religious voice to determine how open the path is to their ideas or how well-crafted the tradition's theologies are to explain existential dilemmas (e.g. what do bad things happen to good people) in a persuasive, cogent way.

Conjunctive Faith
Stage Definition
Mid-life.

This is the stage of reexamining one's faith. If we consider the pattern of change from other religions to Neopaganism, most occur in Young Adulthood or at this stage of life. This is when we often have multiple life experiences that challenge our understanding of reality, from loss to illness to childbirth and fledging one's children. We may also experience crises of relational losses (such as divorce) or financial loss, as well as retirement. If a change does not occur toward another faith, the primary faith is fully integrated in one's life and takes on more important and central meaning. The individual is reflective and often re-imagines the myths and symbols of their faith and crave a deeper more enriched experience. During this stage there is also a greater drive to extend one's faith outward within how they relate to others.

Revised Point: From a religious perspective, this refers to any religious tradition that, while embraces its own definitions, it is open to the views of those of other faiths. It does not seek to position itself as the "sole" truth, but rather as one aspect of truth. We see this embodied in faiths such as Buddhism, various Neopagan traditions and Unitarianism, whereby there is no truth judgments about other faiths. Further there is an emphasis on integrating the elements of challenges, suffering, and life changes into a theological holism.

C Mentoring Tips
When a spiritual mentor encounters someone in this stage, chances are high that the individual has spent a great deal of time reflecting on the nature of their spirituality and concerns. They have likely been situated within the tradition of their choice for many years and are seeking a deeper understanding of their faith and how it serves to help them move through various life transitions. During this time, helping mentees create a new kind of faith narrative that explores how their faith can frame their life lived thus far and lessons learned is critical. Additionally, because this stage also corresponds to the need for a new ap-

proach to social change and engagement with the world, the mentor can also explore with the mentee how to translate their faith into action. This may include ways in which the individual can participate in the world to make it a better place for the next generation, or to encourage the mentee to transform their own role in the faith to become a mentor to individuals just entering the faith.

Inclusive–Generative Faith
Stage Definition
Fowler felt this stage was rarely achieved by any individual and reflects a sense of complete inclusivity of all people and faiths. The individual comes to a sense that all faiths reflect valid meanings. They actively seek to liberate individuals from social oppression and embrace cultural diversity. They are critical about their own faith identifications and often seek to shift areas that have become theologically prone to exclusivity and stagnation. Individuals at this stage are often seen as spiritual inspirations to a wide range of individuals and transcend religious boundaries.

Revised Point: All religions have the potential for manifesting this if they hold a theological position that all religions are inherently valuable. For example, Islam holds a view that all faiths that emerged *prior* to Islam (ranging from shamanism, paganism, Judaism, Christianity, Hinduism, Buddhism, etc.) are of value because their conception of the Divine holds that God does not make faith-based mistakes, rather God revealed its presence over time based on where people were spiritually and psychologically at to receive God. Where this becomes problematic in manifesting this last stage is when Islam is seen as the endpoint for all religious revelation and thus all other religions or new religious movements do not reveal more about the nature of the Divine. In this fashion, any faith-based conception can become inclusive when it theologically acknowledges that all faiths, sustained in diverse human cultures, can illustrate something of value in the nature of the Divine. Further, religions that actively seek to transform exclusionary and prejudicial social practices further manifest this stage of growth.

IG Mentoring Tips
Someone in this position will rarely seek mentoring, other than to help them remain self-reflective and honest. They are likely the ones who are actively transforming their faith and have begun to embrace a global vision of faith. They may step away from any formal religious affiliation

or seek to transform areas of oppression or bias in their religion to encourage an awareness of universal elements of faith.

However, I have also found that many individuals within Neopagan traditions often exhibit this component throughout their growth in the faith. Many active in the Neopagan tradition incorporate principles from diverse religions in their own private practice. In this fashion, when the mentor does in fact encounter elements of this stage, encouraging the individual to develop their own integrative sense of Divine truth can be beneficial. Further it also supports your own growth as a mentor by challenging you to consider diverse religious perspectives and interpretations and to consider how these relate to your own experiences and sense of truth.

Before concluding this section one last note: During the mentoring process, each of your mentees should be approached as a unique individual who may or may not fall easily within any of these stage or process descriptions. When we engage with mentees from the perspective of trying to "fit" them into a stage, we can create conflict and serve to undermine not only our mentoring relationship, but also undermine the degree of bonding that individual is forming to our tradition we are teaching. In this fashion, the stages and processes should be used as guideline to help you process where the individual you are encountering is at in terms of their religious identity and religious development. What you can keep in mind is that individuals grow, like a tree or bush, in relation to their faith. We can approach them as if they are an ornamental bush and thus trim them according to symmetry and sameness so they look like all other members of the tradition or we can be the water and sun that allows the unique branching and shaping to emerge. In this framework, as a mentor, we can in turn become thrilled with the process of discovering our mentee and their rich capacities and their own unique vision of our shared faith that they will ultimately contribute. Through our mentoring actions we can help strengthen their vision and uniqueness, rather than contain it.

Techniques for Mentoring

There are five core mentoring techniques that I tend to advocate. These techniques can be utilized throughout the process of engagement and can generally be adapted at each stage of spiritual development the individual moves within. It's important to recognize the techniques you utilize in the mentoring session should be determined by a careful appreciation and awareness of the needs and abilities of your mentee. Not all mentees are comfortable with performing rituals in the first few encounters with a mentor, because rituals require a certain degree of intimacy and trust between participants—both of which take time to develop. Further not all mentees will want to share elements of their journal and thus the mentor should always allow them the option to disclose what they wish. In this fashion, the spiritual mentor should always be conscious of fostering perfect love and perfect trust within the spiritual mentoring session. This means creating a safe, mentee–centered environment.

Dialoguing

Dialoguing is the most important component of the mentor–mentee relationship. Most of our work with mentees occurs in discussion. The purpose of mentoring is to provide individuals with opportunities to specifically deepen their understanding of their faith, and as such the dialoguing that occurs within the mentoring session should be focused toward the spiritual themes of the tradition and the mentee's spiritual experiences and understanding. We can foster the depth and growth of our mentee by asking open-ended (these are questions that cannot be answered by a yes/no response) questions and presenting theo/alogical concepts for the mentee to engage with. Specifically, when we ask open-ended questions, we should look at developing questions that elicit the mentee's feelings and thoughts. For example:

- How would you define your family-of-origin's religious tradition? (this is a cognitive-based question)

- How do you feel when you consider transitioning into this [Neopagan Tradition]? (emotion-based question)

In developing questions to foster dialogue, the best way to determine the kinds of questions to ask is to reflect on your own experiences with your spiritual development. Consider the following spheres that serve to impact your spiritual development: (a) **time** (your religious past, your religious present, and where you hope your faith will take you); (b) **relational** (how your faith has been impacted by your family of origin, your many current social groups, your relationship to Nature); (c) **meaning** (how your beliefs about the essential meaning of life and the nature of reality have shaped your religious development); and (d) **political–cultural** (consider broader cultural issues that have impacted your spiritual growth). Mentors should always have their own journal to not only process their own spiritual experiences, but also their encounters with mentees. This in turn provides a rich resource for generating questions and determining the success of certain experiential activities used in the process.

When presenting theo/alogical concepts for the mentee to deepen their experience with, the key is to encourage the mentee to personalize and internalize the concepts. For example, if introducing the ethic of "do as you would as long as it doesn't harm anyone"—ask the mentee what this means to them and how might/does it manifest in their day to day life. Are there areas in their life they feel they struggle with maintaining this ethic and what do they perceive are the barriers that challenge it? In this fashion when exploring theo/alogical concepts remember the following steps:

- Introduce the concept as it most commonly emerges in a quote or liturgical prayer (such as "an it harm none, do what ye will", which is the most common appearance within the Wiccan Rede);

- Provide a brief elaboration on the concept—provide alternate ways of expressing the concept, even consider how it emerges in other faiths or in secular (non-religious) environments.

- Ask an open-ended question about how the mentee understands the concept and how it manifest in his or her life; if they are very new to the tradition and have not actively utilized the concept, then ask them how it might manifest in their lives ("what if").

- Once you've heard their response, ask questions that challenge them to "deepen" their understanding or consider having reading material nearby to provide them with to read. Additionally, if it suits the topic consider an experiential ritual to help them gain a deeper understanding.

One final note on questions, avoid asking questions that begin with "why". Research has shown that "why" questions within the interpersonal context tend to place the individual in a defensive position and can be interpreted as carrying a negative judgment. This doesn't mean you won't ask why questions during the mentoring process—trust me, you will—but you should get in the habit of asking questions that begin with "how" or "what". In this capacity, I generally recommend that if you are considering mentoring that you begin with practicing open-ended questions in your day-to-day life. Become aware of when you ask yes/no (closed) questions and consider how you might have asked an open-ended question and what might have been elaborated based on this; also practice getting rid of questions that begins with "why" and see how this impacts your social dialogues.

Journaling

I do not think I have ever encountered work within Neopagan faiths that did not encourage the use of a journal, nor have I ever forgone the recommendation for journaling within my counseling practice. Journals provide a wonderful tool for consistent reflection and to monitor growth. They provide a sense of security and an opportunity for full disclosure, while at the same time helping modify painful and overwhelming emotions into feeling states that can be processed, examined, and released without harm to oneself or one's relationships. The journal within the Neopagan mentoring practice can be a rich tool to facilitate expanded reflection on the elements dialogued during session. Many mentees disclose personal information in the session at different time rates, while they will always disclose their thoughts in a journal—and thus even when you think the mentoring relationship is stalling or your mentee appears more reluctant to communicate, giving the gift of a journal and encouraging writing can keep the work going. There are two ways to work with journals, the first is to assign specific reflection activities, such as writing about one's past religious experiences or journaling about a theo/alogical concept. The second way is to encourage the mentee to write in their journal after every session to reflect on what the session brought out for them and any questions raised in the session. It is often a very good idea to make journal writing a sacred process—encouraging the individual to recognize that taking time to reflect on their faith and their life in relation to their faith is a powerful spiritual experience. I generally recommend that individuals light a candle and say a prayer to a chosen deity they feel is guiding them in their spiritual growth before they begin writing in their journal, then conclude the process with prayer of thanks.

Religious Identity Mapping

This is a specific activity than can be done in a group or during an individual mentoring session and can be done in a very creative way. Mentees are asked to literally map their religious growth they have experienced—they can represent key moments of their life with a range of descriptive words, poetic writing, or images and colors. I also encourage that individuals take time to illustrate and reflect on where they hope their new path will bring them. After the work is completed the mentee can discuss it in the group or during an individual session with their mentor. The mentor then should use dialoguing to help the mentee elaborate and develop a cohesive religious identity narrative. The mentor should pay close attention to areas of anger and conflict or negative past experiences the individual has had with other faith experiences and help them harness forgiveness (forgiveness is often misunderstood as letting someone off the hook from a perceived/actual injustice, quite the contrary; it is about releasing the energy of these experiences so that one no longer suffers from the injustice, this in turn may let them explore problem-solving strategies in a calm and clear manner to redress the injustice) and seeing what strengths they gained from them.

Stage-based Rituals

When mentees do appear to move in a trajectory of development, it's important to celebrate their growth through faith-based rituals that may be public, session-based, or private (mentee engages with them at home). Initiation into a tradition is often the first public ritual mentees will move through, but there can be celebrations of smaller milestones. For example, when a mentee has spent time gaining a firm footing in the intellectual aspects of a theo/alogical aspect, a ritual based in this concept can serve to deepen and internalize this concept.

Deepening Meditations

Guided meditations within the mentoring session can be a wonderful resource for facilitating the deepening awareness of various concepts associated with your tradition. These types of meditations can serve to not only help individuals gain a sense of their spiritual center, but also gain a deeper and transcendental experience of the Divine. These meditations tend to be highly visual and seek to create a certain emotional response. For example, to help individuals experience a sense of oneness with the earth, a popular meditation is becoming the tree, whereby the individual visualizes their legs morphing into roots and borrowing down and their upper bodies stretching and reaching out as trunk and branch. The effective meditation is filled with opportunities for the individual to utilize their imagination to enhance their internalization of the relationship of unity between Earth and Self.

Homework and Reading

There are often key books or myths that are central to a Neopagan tradition or which have been particularly influential to the mentor or the broader Neopagan faith. It's a very good idea to have mentees read outside the mentoring session and journal about their feelings to these texts—then discuss them in the session and how they relate to the individual personally and to their spiritual growth.

Education

What type of education might someone seeking to be a Neopagan mentor need? One of the best forms of education is having been successfully mentored. If you wish to be a mentor, seek out someone who has expertise in your specific Neopagan faith and who has mentored others and ask them to mentor you. This will provide you with practical experience on what works and what might not work. It's important, however, to recognize that your experience with mentoring should not lead to a rigid sense of how to do it that you struggle to relate to the unique aspects of your own mentees. Rather, being mentored (and being mentored while mentoring can be even more rewarding) should create a sounding board and generate ideas rather than become a rule of law.

Mentors require a fair amount of experience within their Neopagan tradition. In this fashion, you should already have a committed sense of faith to your path and have spent several years formally and informally studying. The more you know about the parameters of the faith you are mentoring individuals to engage with, the more effective you will be in certain elements of the mentoring process. In this fashion, before you choose to mentor, take time to assess what you know and what you do not know about your faith. One way to do this corresponds to how scientists engage in writing research. They read until they start reading texts that repeat other texts they've read. Once you get to the point where you are reading texts that refer back to other text's you've already read, then chances are you have a solid foundation in the basic knowledge of your faith. You can also write out your book list then do a search online to see what other traditions recommend for reading and assess if you've read the key foundational books.

The Pedagogy Expert

The pedagogy expert of the pastor role is one that often occurs independent of the full pastoral role and one which we touched upon in the previous chapter's discussion of the "teacher". The pedagogy expert differs from the spiritual mentor in that it is all about teaching concepts and central tenets of the specific Neopagan faith. This is not about deepening spiritual awareness as it is about the pragmatic aspect of learning the parameters of the tradition. There are two primary strategies that Neopagan pastor will manifest this element of the role:

- As a grader and feedback provider—with a variable role in the development of written lessons and homework questions (sometimes this is written by a High Priest or Priestess and graded by those at lower ranks; other times it may be written by those who specialize in the teaching of new members)—this is one of the most common manifestations of this role in the age of increasing distant learning, whereby there is no face-to-face instruction and sometimes little group interaction on the tradition;

- As the primary developer of lessons and direct educator (face to face or fully integrated online classroom site).

If your role primarily consists of feedback and grading, then it is important to make sure the feedback you give is not simply "excellent". Ask questions of what the individual wrote or extend their thought processes to a different direction. Additionally highlight statements that capture the essence of the lesson or the topic to help encourage thinking along those lines. Recognize, too, that sometimes students will not provide adequate responses—return it to them with clear information about where elaboration should occur or ask them to respond to your feedback with greater elaboration.

It's important to recognize that not all individuals are adept at written responses. If your tradition focuses on writing and the successful completion of written modules and you have a student who is not succeeding, consider either modifying your program to verbal responses if possible or refer the individual to a face-to-face environment that may be more conducive to their learning style.

Second, also consider the purpose of the written work as well. If the purpose is for an advanced degree—seminary training for example—then the work is designed to highlight those who will be adept at teaching and scholarly roles within a faith. If the purpose is to orient individuals into a religious life as an adherent, then emphasizing successful completion of written reports may exclude individuals who have strong faith and would benefit from a Neopagan community. In other words, not everyone deserving to be involved in a faith *must be a successful "student"*. In this fashion, taking time to assess how open or closed your faith-based group is along dimensions of academic skill should be assessed for consistency with Neopagan religious ethics of inclusivity.

When your role is the developer and primary educator of lessons, then you need to know the goals of your tradition and what constitutes knowledge requirements at each stage of development. For example if you teach Wicca and maintain the degree-based program, than you should know what are the key theo/alogical milestones for each degree that individuals must know to successfully complete it. Additionally, you also need to know a little about how people learn and strategies to intervene to encourage learning.

A Brief Guide to Teaching Techniques

Learning is the process by which we acquire knowledge. When we have learned something it becomes permanent. Learning is something that all living brains are designed to do—learning is how we adapt and cope with the changes in our environment and ultimately promotes our survival. When we focus our discussion to Neopagan students, the goal is about permanently learning the concepts and liturgical rites of the specific Neopagan tradition we are working within. This often includes wider learning of other religious traditions and theological concepts to ensure the student is able to situate Neopaganism within the broad field of religion. In this fashion, the pedagogically minded Neopagan pastor is conscious of what the topical parameters are for each student to successfully master before moving further in their faith. That defines the *what* that is learned. Yet, *how* do students learn? When we consider how students learn we are talking about three things: how material to be learned is introduced to the prospective student (acquisition of material); the context of the learning environment (where individuals learn); and memory.

Memory

The most fundamental aspect of learning is memory—to learn something means to be able to remember it over the long haul. Memory is broken three parts: Sensory memory, Short-term memory and Long-term. As a teacher, you need to know how to move information through these stages to long-term memory.

Sensory memory is defined as the first step in processing information and refers to our encounter with visual, tactile, olfactory, kinesthetic (physical), taste, and auditory exposure to the information coming in. These events are initially captured as purely sensory experiences devoid of any contextual meaning. Holding as many as 10 items for each 1/20th of a second, this information is quickly shunted into the brain for short-term memory processing. We are unconscious (that is not aware) of this layer of processing (it is also one of the rationales for subliminal advertising, which actually doesn't work because unless individuals use *conscious* or *conditional* learning responses chances are high that the information won't make it to long-term memory and thus lead to a behavioral change). It's important to note that in order to have sensory memory, the student must be able to attend to the stimulus (what is being presented to the student for learning)—thus attention must be achieved—more on this in the next section.

Short-term memory is the allocation of space in the brain (and memory is actually stored throughout the brain not in any one region) for brief storage of information. Generally the most individuals can retain at any given time are 7 units of information—this can be 7 individual numbers or 7 chunked elements (groups of material that go together easily). Information held in STM can be quickly replaced if new information is given too soon before information can be *learned* (transferred to Long-term memory). If you do not rehearse the information that has just arrived from your sensory memory, within 15 to 30 seconds you will have forgotten in.

Long-term memory is permanent neural networks established in the brain dedicated to retaining information over the long haul. Researchers generally divide LTM between episodic (information related to your life—the where, who, when, and how of memories) and semantic (the *what*: words, facts, grammar, etc.). In research many individuals often use "I remember" when prefacing recall of an episodic memory; and "I know" when prefacing recall of semantic memory.

In addition to knowing the way in which memory is stored, we also need to know how this process unfolds. Memory storage or formation occurs in three broad steps that are critical for assessing any learning difficulties a student is having and developing strategies to encourage retention.

Encoding refers to the step where the memory is created. Once information transfers from the sensory to the STM, it has developed a cohesive set of properties and potential associations with other memories you already have. When information fails to encode, you have never learned it—it's simply information that hit your senses and may have briefly remained in your STM, but then dissipates. Students with attentional issues will often have difficulty with encoding—a teacher then needs to explore new ways to gain attention.

Storage—once the memory has formed it is moved to the LTM for long-term storage. When we learn information, we are in effect storing it for later use.

Retrieval refers to the capacity of retrieving that stored memory for use. We can learn many things, but if we can't pull them back out of our neurological file cabinet for use, there's not much point. In fact, problems in retrieval are often critical challenges for students. Teachers then need to be able to give students several types of cues (triggers for retrieving) to help access this information (cues are often designed to replicate some element of the initial environment the items were learned in or related information that the student may have linked in their neural file cabinet [e.g feathers as a cue for bird])

Acquisition

Acquisition refers to how we gain and retain knowledge. There are two primary ways in which we can develop our capacity to remember specific information. **Shallow processing** is repetition—repeating a concept or a word or a skill over and over again. The down side of this method of acquiring knowledge: it also tends to be passive, that is the student doesn't actively "think" about what they are doing. This can be an effective way to learn a complex motor skill like an instrument, but does little for learning facts and conceptual information. Many students undermine their learning through repetition of definitions when studying—information learned through this type of processing generally does not last and may not readily be retrieved during a test.

A second and very important type of acquiring information is **elaborative rehearsal**. Elaborative processing is one of the most important skills a student can engage with to learn and something a teacher can readily foster. Elaborative rehearsal is active and involves students exploring the material in greater depth. For example, concept maps is a form of elaborative rehearsal whereby the key concept is placed in a center bubble and the students and teacher generate related concepts by attaching them to the bubble. The more related concepts the student develops to literally elaborate their understanding of the concept the more likely they will remember the concept over time. Further, the advantage of elaboration—relating the material to be learned to other material already learned—the easier it is to retrieve that material later because you are increasing the number of key images, words, and concepts that are *encoded* in the initial memory—you then have more cues. Any strategy that encourages students to personalize, engage with, and expand their understanding of the concepts through their own cognitive power increases the likelihood of remembering the material.

Finally, a last word on acquisition and factors associated with the learner that can inhibit learning: mood and neurocognitive difficulties. Students who experience depression and anxiety have less available cognitive energy to remember information. It's neurologically exhausting to cope with anxiety and depression and can significantly inhibit the ease with which students will learn. If you are working with a Neopagan student coping with severe depression or anxiety, it's important to encourage them to seek counseling support to help reduce these affective responses *before* beginning the learning process. If they are already in the process, be sure to encourage them to be patient with themselves and to recognize it can take more time to get all the information. Keep in mind that you, too, will need to model patience and acceptance and support. Finally students with neurocognitive issues such as Attention Deficit Disorder or other learning-based disabilities need some flexibility built into the learning process. If learning through auditory means (talking concepts aloud) doesn't seem to be working, try developing a written lesson or vice versa. Additionally consider using sound or visual depictions as alternatives to written and oral. Above all patience is the key.

Context

For years, the education field never thought much about the environment students learned in. We now know the context in which one learns can play a huge role in how well one will actually remember. Environments that are high in judgment, punishment, and authoritarian in nature (the teacher is in charge and discourages dialogue between students or self) can significantly reduce learning success of students. Students experience greater stress in these environments coupled with less opportunities for a sense of success, in turn students demonstrate lower retention rates and higher reports of hopelessness and pessimism in their capacity to succeed. Environments where the teacher presents information in creative ways but is emotionally disengaged or inaccessible or provides little or no feedback will also reduce retention. However, environments where students are encouraged to work cooperatively together whereby the teacher encourages students to actively work as co-creators of knowledge—as "explorers" in search of greater clarity, have students who succeed most of the time in the environment. In this fashion, if you are teaching Neopagan students, a group is the best option coupled with encouraging students to work cooperatively to elaborate and explore concepts. Be sure to ensure that all students engage in the dialogue and set the tone that their thoughts are all valuable.

The next aspect of context is *how* information is presented. The more senses students have to use to process material, the more likely they will have a richly encoded memory and thus greater options for retrieval. A good example of this process at work is within Neopagan rituals that are often physical (tactile and kinesthetic) in their ritual movements; olfactory in their use of incense, fragrant oils and herbs; visual in their use of ritual objects and symbols; auditory in their use of chanting, signing, drumming and speaking; in their use of taste through the sharing of communal cakes and wine; and imaginal—requiring students to create internal mental images of the circle. In this rich context of full sensory involvement, students not only can have a literal "visceral" experience, but also remember this for later use. In this capacity, when you, as a teacher, can create rich experiential moments to illustrate concepts you wish the students to learn, you increase the likelihood of their remembering.

Finally knowledge learned must be able to **transfer** to other circumstances. If you can only remember a certain concept in Neopaganism within the room you learned it, then it does very little good at impacting the whole of your life. We encode information based on where we learn it—for example, if you have to take a test in biology, studying in the classroom you'll be taking it in will increase the likelihood of remembering the information. However, if you only study in this classroom and then take another course related to it, you'll likely have to relearn much of the information because it won't transfer. It's stuck, literally, in the room. In this capacity, learning the same information in several contexts can increase the robustness of your memory and capacity to retrieve it as needed. As such, as a Neopagan teacher, it can be a good idea to teach a concept in different settings. For example, let's say you are teaching the concept of birth–death–regeneration. This concept can be introduced within your meeting place or your online environment, but then you can either assign or lead a Nature walk where this concept is explored in Nature. You can also have students volunteer at a hospital or go to a store to watch how this concept might manifest in cultural lives of people.

Putting It Together

You do not need to be trained as a teacher to be a teacher. The key is to reflect on how you have learned information and what has worked and what has not worked. Reflecting on our own time as a student can help us determine strategies that can be effective for teaching. You *do* need to know the key concepts and liturgical structures for the level of education your students are at. In this capacity, you do need to be an expert in what knowledge is necessary. So how do you put this all together?

1. Define the critical milestones for your tradition—what are students expected to achieve over the long haul?

2. Break these milestones into achievable parts, keep in mind that students can remember 7 related chunks of information in any given learning situation—keeping it simple, keeps it achievable.

3. Reflect on your own learning experience—what teaching methods worked for you and what didn't. Consider your own past experience and how this matches with your own lesson levels—do you need to make changes and break them down more?

4. Take time to assess how your students learn—ask them about their past learning experiences and what made their previous teachers successful or not, what academic subjects did they excel in, where did they struggle and why? Taking time to have your students share with you and each other their own learning experiences can go a long way in shaping your lessons.

5. When you begin to teach concepts think about how you can incorporate more senses and be sure to allow students to elaborate on them. Give homework that allows students to apply their knowledge in other contexts or to consider how the concepts relate to other elements of

their life outside of Neopaganism.

6. When you assess students in their success, be sure to look at your own. Adjust your teaching interventions based on the needs of the students—we are all students ultimately and thus can benefit from change.

The Counselor

Neopagan Pastoral Counseling is known as *supportive counseling* and is a relationship designed to help individuals adjust to the challenges we all face or could face in our lives through the framing of these events within the symbols, stories, and meanings of the Neopagan faith. In this fashion, the Neopagan counselor situates the issues the individual is experiencing within the context of Neopagan models of meaning and development. It may include rituals to promote healing or a greater connection of the divine; and it may also include assigning reading material to help foster self-help and growth.

However, Neopagan Pastoral Counseling is not the same as psychotherapy. Pastoral counseling should *never* be the primary method of treatment for individuals experiencing significant mental health crisis[9]. Unlike other elements of the Priest and Priestess role the counseling role requires having experience and knowing your limitations. If you do not have training and supervision by an elder with pastoral counseling experience, do not take on this responsibility. Now, let's look at some specifics of pastoral counseling.

The Pastoral Counseling Relationship

A positive and healing counseling relationship contains several essential elements:

Respect and empowerment is defined as the counselor's ability to believe in the counselee's resiliency, decision-making, and being able to simply sit and listen to their struggles and challenges without becoming paternalistic (taking charge and telling the person what to do). With respect we believe in and encourage our client's sense of agency and their ability to shape their own life in the way that resonates most truthfully for them.

Unconditional positive regard[10] is the capacity of the counselor to accept the individual sitting with them as they are. We all are imperfect and we all have different ways of seeing the world, most individuals experience distress because those around them have become intolerant to what is unique and different in that individual. The pastoral counselor is responsible for extending themselves in love toward all individuals. This does not mean that as the relationship develops you do not confront the individual if their behavior is harmful to self or others and thus undermines their own agency and capacity for a fulfilling life.

Empathy[11] is our capacity to understand what others are feeling and to accept the full range of their emotions that emerge within a counseling session. We are able to recognize the elements of their situation that are giving rise to their emotions and we refrain from telling them what they should feel or moving them to quickly into action plans. We are also particularly aware of our own level of comfort with hearing their feelings—it is critical not to project (push, displace) our own feelings and thoughts onto the client.

Genuineness refers to our capacity to be authentic and honest with our clients.

Trust refers to our own promise to our clients to retain confidentiality and establish a healthy and accepting holding environment (meaning we don't get flustered or upset when our clients are angry or in despair or any of the any uncomfortable emotions). There are limits to what can be confidential under the laws and so we also are upfront with clients regarding this. Such limitations are: if the individual makes a statement of harming themselves or others, or is engaged in child or elder abuse. Most states require the notification of the police under these events. However, when clients know upfront the limits of confidentiality it can go a long way to building a sense of perfect trust.

Techniques

To get you started thinking about the pastoral counseling role, there are a few key techniques. First is the capacity to be an **active listener**. This means the client you are working with *knows* you are listening. In most circumstances, being truly heard can be the primary cause for effective change for an individual. Most of us are not fully heard in our day-to-day life—and many conflicts we experience often emerge because individuals fail to listen. So how does one listen?

Pay attention—sit face front to the person you are talking with and keep your arms uncrossed over your chest. An open heart position communicates you are receiving the person and unafraid of their emotions—it bolsters their confidence. Keep focused on what they are saying and how their body language is manifesting. Don't let your own life issues distract you—in the Neopagan session, consider preparing yourself

before your client arrives by a simple meditation and making the experience a sacred act.
- Communicate nonverbally and with prompts that you are listening—nod your head, "uh-huhs", allow their feelings to impact you so that your face mirrors their own, and when the individual is shy or nervous, smile to encourage. Remember to be non-threatening!
- **Summarize, Reflect, Clarify**. Summarize what the client has just told you to ensure not only that you got it all right, but to communicate you heard them. Reflect on what you've said with I-statements, "I feel…" "I wonder…" "As I listened, I couldn't help but think of…" as well as reflect on what they've said, "Thinking about what you've experienced, it seems to me that…". Ask questions when you aren't certain about what they are saying, such as "I heard [this]…is that what you are saying?" These are the primary skills for **any** good counselor to ensure their client knows they are being heard and that you know what is being communicated.
- **Religious interventions**—only after a client has been allowed to fully express their feelings should you begin to look at religious elements of their story. It should never be done in a way that undermines the authentic emotions—for example, you should never say "you shouldn't feel angry because…". Rather, tell stories that demonstrate the positive outcome from the negative experience the individual is in—thus instilling hope and optimism. For example, a Neopagn member comes to you having just left a violent relationship and is torn, you might wish to talk about and even engage in a ritual associated with Artemis or Athena—goddesses that retain their singleness and are also warriors in their own right.
- Your work isn't over when the session is done. You MUST process (reflect and consider future interactions and directions) the interaction either in a journal or with an elder supervisor. Taking time to ceremonial close the session to release the emotions is also important to keep your own health.

༄

Regardless of which pastoral role you pursue, the key to remember is the centrality of your students. Within the pastoral role, in all three of its manifestations, the core element is service. In this fashion, in all role elements, our primary question is: *How can I serve my student or my community better?* It is not about ego or being the center of attention. If you find that you take things personally and feel compelled to move students into your values and beliefs, then a pastoral role is not for you. Pastors check their egos at the door and encounter each student with a sincere desire to learn who that person is and how they uniquely see the world and what they need from the faith to help them more fully love and live their life. It is a role that should be entered into after deep reflection, not simply on your skill level, but your emotional and relational readiness.

6
Power & Confidentiality

Power

Philosopher Michel Foucault proposed power had certain properties. First, he defined power as centrally linked to knowledge "truths". In this fashion, Foucault suggested in order for any one individual to *have* power they first must assert some knowledge–truth claim. Second, Foucault proposed power is never a centralized concept thus it cannot be linked to any one individual, but rather circulates through organizations. As such no one individual has power, rather power is disseminated *between* people in specific ways—these specific ways have to do with how an individual *relates* to or embodies their cultural roles. In this capacity, a parent has power not because of the characteristics of the individual, but because of the characteristics and social meaning of the parenting role. Finally, Foucault states power is neutral, becoming positive or negative depending on how it is used and who is doing the perceiving of the outcomes of power.[1] Under Foucault's definition, power has the following qualities:

1. Asserts itself through truth/knowledge claims;

2. Emerges within a social context and meaning; and

3. Is neither a positive or negative until it is deployed and perceived.

However, Foucault does not necessarily define what power is. For this, we can turn to another philosopher, Rosabeth Moss Kanter, who defines power as "the ability to mobilize resources to achieve self-determined ends".[2] Her own definition is markedly different from Foucault in that she ignores the social context, meaning, and truth claims; however she does suggest that power can be defined as an ability—the capacity to mobilize resources to achieve goals. As such, to gain a complete definition of power we can include the personal of Kanter's definition with the public–social definition of Foucault. In this capacity, power can be defined as:

> the ability to achieve and mobilize social and material resources through the assertion and utilization of truth claims and social position (both creating authority) to meet one's[3] goals.

The challenge of power, however, is that if we adhere to Foucault's value-free definition of power, whereby power is neither inherently positive nor negative but dependent on perception, it can lead moral relativism (that is no moral consensus). That is we can never claim certain uses of power or certain structures that create power are inherently problematic. What makes this value-free position challenging is that in order for individuals to *have* or *acquire* power they must have *access* to social contexts that support power. We know from social justice research to have access to a social context that supports power is not value-free or neutral—but a question of *privilege* that is often based on bias and prejudicial assumptions that decide which group or which individuals morally deserve to have power while excluding others from such positions. One of the most glaring issues of privileging and access to power that many Neopagans can readily see is the way in which Western society grants greater power and thus resources (such as political, legal, monetary, social acceptance, and the right to publically acknowledge one's faith) to Christians *over* other faiths, particularly Neopagan traditions. In order for this privileging to occur, Christianity must be first perceived and viewed as the morally superior faith, while other faiths are by degree seen as morally inferior. In this fashion, as we begin to explore power within the context of the role as priest and priestess, we must explore it under several perspectives:

- How is power established within the social contexts?

- Who is privileged to become a priest/ess and by contrast who is excluded, if any?

- How does the priest or priestess assert/demonstrate their power through truth and knowledge claims?

- How does the priest or priestess define and utilize their resources to achieve their specific goals within the context of their professional role?

- What are the parameters between the individual goals of the priest/priestess and the worshiping community they serve? What is the nature of the power relationship between the priest/priestess and the worshiping community?

- How is power dispersed within the worshipping community?

The Social–Contextual Establishment

Neopaganism is a de-privileged faith worldwide. While there has been a movement in Westernized nations to promote religious diversity, many Neopagans still practice their faith in the privacy of their own home or in the safety of anonymous online groups to protect themselves from public scrutiny and discrimination. In this fashion, Neopaganism does not have access to significant sources of social authority and power that other faiths, such as Christianity have. And there may be a benefit from this lack of access in that Neopaganism is unlikely to assert its truth claims by widely institutionalizing harmful or discriminatory behavior that not only harms adherents, but poses a risk to those who worship outside the faith. Yet, while Neopaganism does not gain the direct benefits of privilege other faiths enjoy (ability to practice openly, access to federal dollars to support educational or associated faith-based initiatives, legal protection, and social acceptance), its position as being an outsider does have its own source of power. Specifically, it's structured in a *power-against* relationship.[4]

In the power-against relationship a de-privileged group or individual mobilizes resources to transform a power-over[5] relational structure. Through the process of coming together, individuals engage in resistance practices against the status quo—the accepted power arrangements in society. This becomes a source of individual power (known as *empowerment,* whereby individuals who practice Neopaganism may feel vulnerable alone begin to feel encouraged and emboldened in their membership to a group, thus a larger power source) and strengthens the collective power of the group—the more members the more social authority emerges. As such the first layer of power, the Neopagan Priest or Priestess engages with is the issue of reclaiming[6] power.

Reclaiming is a loaded term. On one hand, it implies the act of taking back. For most Neopagans, this is the act of reasserting the spiritual validity of pagan practices of antiquity that have been oppressed or extinguished in favor of a mono- or all-encompassing faiths (often Christianity, although this is only true in Western civilization, but not true in all cultures who have denied Neopagan and related folk-based practices). Thus it is the act of taking back the right to practice faiths that have otherwise been deemed heretical or otherwise silenced. On the other hand, it is also about asserting the contemporary right to religious freedom. Often Neopagans are at the heart of religious freedom cases, particularly in the Western world, but increasingly in other regions such as South Africa and the Middle East. Through the process of reclaiming, Neopagans redefine and rewrite the value judgments and biases that have otherwise demeaned and deprivileged their faith beliefs.

When we apply this to the role of priest or priestess, we find the power position of reclaiming is a weighty one. It means that the public role of Neopagan Priest or Priestess is one that requires continuous assertion against the religious mainstream status quo. This does not mean that each priest and priestess must engage in political or public action, but it does mean that their social power lies in how well they understand the issue of reclaiming and how well they can re-situate their own tradition as a valuable and integral part of human religious endeavors. The challenge for the priest and priestess is not to become like other dominant faiths, who gain their label "dominant" because they dominate the religious discourse and make absolute truth claims at the exclusion of other faiths.

When we interpret power as the capacity to mobilize resources, the priest or priestess can utilize their underdog position to encourage members to engage in personally and socially empowering acts. For example, Goddess practitioner and editor of *The Beltane Papers* Lisé Quinn[7] featured a lengthy article on the reasons why voting was of central importance to Neopagans. Specifically, she notes that voting ensures continued legal power and protection from discrimination—to keep those of the dominant faiths that would otherwise oppress pagan practices. Voting, in Quinn's article, was literally equal to "the power to make social change", writing "social change is only possible when we stand up to be counted". Thus in Quinn's article she emphasizes the underdog position of Neopagans and provides one avenue in which this position can serve to inspire adherents to stand *against* the power structures in the majority and thus reclaim power—or claim more power.

Does this mean that every priest or priestess must be prepared to lead their adherents into political causes? Not really—and definitely not if you have a tax exemption status as it is ultimately illegal to use your spiritual and religious authority (power) to influence adherent's political views. What it does mean is the priest and priestess recognizes that this is the foundation of their power and manifests it fully. The priest and priestess are able to stand against[8] social structures that are oppressive and through the act of standing against, they are able to inspire and obtain greater social power for their adherents. What is important, however, is the priest or priestess is comfortable with the responsibility of being the standard bearer. Additionally, the priest and priestess should also know how their own fear (and disempowerment) of their underdog social power position impacts how they feel about themselves and their faith. For example, many African American men and women of the pre-Civil Rights movement often felt profound (and justified) fear of White America and encouraged their children to keep their heads down and try not to draw attention to oneself for fear of violent reprisals. The challenge of holding on to these habits is that it prohibits social change—if the victims of racisms cannot stand up—those in charge certainly will not change. The same holds for a woman who is raped—if she does not speak out, nothing will change. In this capacity, our own fears associated with speaking out, being noticed, and standing up to be counted can undermine the power of our faith, its members, and perpetuate disempowerment and victimization. Society only changes when those who have been oppressed stand *against* the structures of oppression. Thus as a priest or priestess it is critical that you explore your own fears of social repercussions *before* taking on a leadership position. Consider reading books about historical leaders past and present such as Ghandi, Martin Luther King Jr., Malcolm X, Fredrick Douglas, Abraham Lincoln, Alice Walker, bell hooks, Elizabeth Cady Stanton, Barack Obama, Dorothea Dix, and other leaders who have had to confront damaging power structures from positions of disempowerment and how they did it.

Privileging: Inclusion & Exclusion in Neopaganism

While Neopaganism is a faith that is in a less privileged power position than other faiths, it does have its own ways of privileging (of including) and de-privileging (of excluding) others that needs to be understood. Most (not all) Neopagan traditions have a clergy system—that is a closed[9] hierarchical structure of authority. In this fashion, having a clergy system centrally means that not everyone will have access to the same sources of power—the same resources. It is important to recognize this issue in that to be of the clergy means to have *more* power than those who are not in the clergy. Typical sources of power allocated only to the clergy include the decisional capacity to determine ritual protocol, the capacity to determine and define beliefs, the capacity to accept or decline members both to the clergy or as worshipping members, access to educational resources (often described as "mysteries" or "secret knowledge" that non-clergy members are not taught), direct monetary benefits, and maintaining the overall rules and day-to-day functions of the faith.

This does not mean that Neopaganism is itself exclusionary. It is actually a constellation of faiths that is typically much more inclusionary than other religious traditions. Members are not denied based on political or social views, gender, ethnicity, sexual orientation, ablebodiness etc. Rather most Neopagan traditions embrace new members from a wide range of perspectives. However, exclusion does occur and it is the clergy's responsibility to continuously assess:

- *Who* is being excluded and *who* is being included?

- For what reasons is the exclusion occurring?
- Are such practices potentially beneficial to the community and in what ways?
- How are such practices harmful to the community and in what ways? and
- Are such justifications for the exclusion in keeping with the ethics of the faith?

Some examples of problematic areas of exclusion and assessment may revolve around money or education. For example, a group charges a hefty fee for membership per year; this may ensure that well-off individuals (who are already resource-powerful in mainstream society) to dominate the group and the group's ethical and theological framework (thus the groups perceptions). At the same time this group would ultimately exclude individuals who may lack financial resources and thus also have less social power (and who would ultimately benefit more from a community resource). The exclusion of these individuals would also typically lead to the loss of more diverse theological perspectives, goals, and ideas. Another possible situation that could occur would be exclusions based on education—while this might be less likely in an actual coven setting; groups that operate to mirror a more rigorous academic environment, might limit membership only to college graduates, thus closing the door to a large number of qualified individuals within the Neopagan arena and again the potential for theological expansion and growth.

In this capacity, it is important to keep in mind that what will define your resources and thus your power depends on who is included and who is excluded from your tradition. Because inclusion and exclusion often occur, not because of truly valid definitions of difference or incompatibility, but because of stereotyping and bias, it is critical that priests and priestesses carefully examine their policies of exclusion and the degree of matching with the ethical values of their Neopagan faith. For example, if your tradition values outright equality of all individuals, than exclusions of any type can be problematic and that includes even maintaining a clergy. In this fashion, the priest and priestess should take time to assess who is allowed to belong and who is not and to carefully consider the benefits of this inclusion/exclusion pattern and assess whether it is theologically appropriate. As an added note, the more diversity embraced within a group, the stronger the group will become and the more likely they will deepen not only theological concepts, but how these concepts may be applied to everyday life.

Truth & Knowledge Claims

Authority is typically established by asserting knowledge claims. For example, our Western culture typically ascribes greater social power to those with educational degrees than those without—the primary reason for this is the assumption that education is synonymous with greater knowledge. Hence Francis Bacon's famous quote *"knowledge is power"*. When we apply this to religion two specific issues emerge:

1. Knowledge authority that is implied or explicitly claimed by the priest/ess;

2. Truth claims about the specific tradition's beliefs on how the universe works, who's in charge, and how we should lead our lives based.

The priest/ess by claiming this title has overtly claimed knowledge and thus authority. What is implied by the title is the type of knowledge claimed by the individual, most commonly theological and liturgical knowledge. The title implies the individual has achieved some form of education to be able to teach and minister to members of a similar faith. In Neopaganism legitimate knowledge sources that allow a person to be called this title can vary. For example, a person may have been literally taught their tradition by spirit guides and ancestors—thus they are initiated into the clergy by the spirits themselves (as seen in shamanistic paths or when a new faith springs up unrelated to any other). Another member may have substantially read on their chosen faith, crafted their tradition based on integrating aspects of what they have read and experienced, and then achieved ordination through an interfaith organization without initiating into any specific tradition. Another member may have attended a seminary where they formally studied their faith through a mixture of scholarly and experiential methods and engaged in a supervised internship before being conferred a title. Still another member may have initiated into a specific Neopagan tradition and thus has garnered their title following immersion and acceptance in a specific path. What this ultimately means is that within Neopaganism there are many legitimate paths to acquiring knowledge authority. Whether all adherents will accept your knowledge path as legitimate will depend on how they define what constitutes knowledge authority in their own definition of Neopaganism. Truth claims within Neopaganism are similarly diverse.

Most religious faiths outside of Neopaganism hold that their faith is the only "true" way of seeing and connecting to the Divine and living a morally spiritual life. This has often inspired much of the religious rhetoric of who is saved during periods of judgment—thus those who follow the "true" faith will experience a joyous reunion with the Divine, while all others will experience retribution. Neopaganism is uniquely different in that it does not ascribe to any type of them/us duality, whereby individuals in another faith are somehow less than or uninspired or not divine. Rather, Neopaganism typically asserts a truth claim that *all* individuals are divine and that the presence of the Divine is both *within* all of us and *without* (thus around all of us, shaping us). Because this is an inclusive rather than exclusive truth, Neopagans typically do not feel a competitive need to draw cultural boundaries of us versus them. Nevertheless, this is a truth claim and as such becomes a *powerful* source for influencing an adherent's behavior. Further because Neopaganism often sees *truth* in all faiths—that is all faiths reveal something of the divine—there is a tendency to embrace or even overtly incorporate religious teachings and texts from other faiths. Thus we can also see that the truth claim increases the resources for the Neopagan adherent to use when addressing life challenges and faith-based issues—thus Neopaganism actively seeks to *increase* its power through increasing its theological resources. This drive also increases the knowledge of the adherents—many Neopagans tend to be highly educated about world religions, often having read a number of current and historical religious texts and religious commentary.

Personal Power of the Priest and Priestess

As briefly touched upon in the previous section, the priest and priestess have specific resources for power that differ from the adherents or non-clergy in their faith. They have greater power than these members because they have a greater number of resources from which to draw. Briefly, the priest and priestess typically have the following sources of power:

- The right to define, alter, and create theological beliefs;

- The capacity to accept or decline members for worship;

- The right to officiate all ritual/liturgical elements of worship;

- The capacity to remove any member or lower-leveled clergy from office or the worship group;

- The ability to set the tone for the dynamics between members;

- The ability to determine who is qualified for initiation or teaching and who is not;

- Access to mystery or hidden/non-public knowledge adherents do not have;

- Access to financial reimbursement for time, teaching, and counseling;

- Legal recognition of authority conferred by title to oversee marriage and death rites, as well as participate in pastoral care; and

- Ego resources, such as a sense of greater control and capacity conferred through holding the other power resources as well as in the role of being sought out by other members for help, guidance, or teaching.

In contrast, non-clergy members in a Neopagan group do not have these resources and may further, depending on the structure of the relationship and the degree of power sharing (sharing resources), lack confidence to develop their own theological and personally relevant spiritual identity. They may become preoccupied with being wrong or not doing things right or become fixated on the material elements of the faith, rather than the spiritual elements if the priest/priestess misuses their power "authoritatively" (paternalistically or engaging in behavior without allowing members to experiment, engage, or otherwise comment on the process). In this fashion, the priest and priestess needs to be very aware of how they utilize these powers within their engagement with their members and engage in ongoing reflexivity (looking at their actions from a position of an outsider) to assess if they are "abusing" their authority.

The Structure of Power:
The Relationship of the Priest/ess to the Community

Power leads to embedded power structures—patterned ways in which individuals relate to each other over time. Within the priest and priestess relationship with the community there are two dominant ways in which power may be structured: (a) power-over and (b) power-with

In the **power-over** relationship the priest/ess has the authority over the members of their tradition. This is a truly embedded hierarchical structure, whereby the priest/ess is seen as the primary authority figure (if not overseen by a High Priest/ess). When this structured relationship is healthy, the resources of the priest/priestess (often their "knowledge" and "truth" resources) are extended to the membership. They in turn are able to learn about their faith and actively contribute to its expansion. When it is unhealthy, the priest/ess assumes a leadership role that is closed and inflexible and asserts their beliefs as the *only* acceptable beliefs. In turn they may actively restrict knowledge or may only provide knowledge to individuals who do certain things for them—this in turn may foster competition between members who seek greater privileging by the priest/ess.

Power-with relationship emerges when power is shared or equal. Generally this will emerge in a Neopagan tradition that does not have a priest/ess caste system. In other words, the tradition is equally shaped by all members. Modified power-with relationships may occur in a priest/ess relationship if they overtly invite members to participate in the establishment and development of the tradition and take a more backseat role in requiring students to match their own beliefs. In other words, the priest/ess may encourage members to fully express their beliefs and provide only minimal feedback. The risk with this power structure can be a lack of order or the lack of development of a consistent and cohesive religious identity. But this should not preclude exploring this type of power structure.

The Dispersal of Power

The dispersal of power means how power moves from the priest/ess to the members. Traditionally, power in Neopaganism is dispersed through the sharing of knowledge, the participation in rituals, and even in the actual raising of power within ritual processes. Additionally, the priest/ess retains a certain degree of openness and flexibility that affords dispersal. In this fashion, the priest/ess remains focused toward sharing with members their knowledge in unrestrictive fashion. Generally, the priest/ess avoids secrecy (either failing to disclose information as "restrictive" or disclosing only to some members over others or requiring members to retain more secrecy than what is reasonable). Through these mechanisms, power (resources) becomes shared among the membership.

Confidentiality

We briefly touched on confidentiality as a method of developing trust within the pastoral relationship. In this section we'll talk more about the specifics of confidentiality within the religious setting. One of the first elements of confidentiality to understand is that it reflects the process of a right to have the information you disclose kept in confidence—kept private. When we disclose information that is personal in nature (ranging from our financial information to private information about our lives) we are giving trust to the other person to keep this information secure. As a priest or priestess you agree to keep your member's personal information secure and safe—thus by extension you convey to them that you are a source of security and safety for their whole person. This also means you never disclose information about a member in the group to another member.

Confidentiality is a power issue. When individuals confide in you personal information, they are giving you something about themselves they do not want others to necessarily know. Further confidentiality between a priest/ess and member is often one-way, whereby the member tells you something rather than equal disclosure. In this capacity, confidentiality supports the process of developing a power-over relationship that must be carefully monitored for temptation. Just think about how many criminal cases have emerged because individuals have used private information to extort resources for their own gain. It can be tempting to breach confidentiality boundaries in favor of extorting power if a member frustrates you or leaves the group. As such it is critical before you allow yourself to become a source of confidence for members that you are ministering to understand just what type of a dream-keeper you are.

- Are you someone who tells everyone all about yourself without reservation—this could lead to disclosing inadvertently about those you know;

- Are you someone who has difficulty keeping personal confidences—you just simply can't keep a secret;

- Are you someone who confides everything to a close friend or significant other without considering how well they keep a secret;

- Are you someone who has utilized private and personal information about another person to harm them, obtain revenge, or even seek to mediate a problem for them;

Are you someone who has engaged in gossiping or frequently engages in it? A yes to any of these questions should give you pause *before* you allow members of your faith to confide in you. As a priest/priestess breaching confidentiality not only undermines their rights and their faith, but also undermines your own authority to be a priest/ess. Within Neopaganism, it is also a violation of *perfect love, perfect trust* ethics. An excellent question to journal about in terms of your ability to keep confidences is: *under what circumstances in the past have I been unable to keep confidentiality or privacy of another individual?*

We all have certain things that make us need to talk. This raises the issue of can we ever process our experiences with another without breeching confidentiality? Yes by following several simple steps:

1. Avoid names and any key identifying markers of a person, such as where they live, went to school or any unique interests; optionally change key elements of the story to make the individual's identity hidden;

2. Ideally never discuss information about another member with *any* member of your community. Ideally, talk with another priest/ess from another coven or discuss your issues with a High Priest/ess (or trusted clergy) or if necessary an individual unrelated to the group who can keep confidence and provide helpful advice.

Finally, one last word before concluding our chapter: There are three specific situations where confidentiality is no longer viable (which we touched on in the previous chapter)—where it is limited: (a) report of child or elder abuse; (b) report of a threat of harm to another person; and (c) report of self-harm. Each of these should be reported to local authorities. And members should always be reminded that, while you prize confidentiality, these three situations do not fall in that parameter. Otherwise, all other types of communication should remain held in confidence.

7
Sex & Multiple Relationships

Multiple Relationships

Multiple relationships emerge when a priest or priestess has other types of relationships with his or her religious community members or their families beyond the ministerial one. This may include being a member's priest/ess as well as their close friend or business partner or being romantically involved with a member. Multiple relationships are one of the most challenging ethical issues to negotiate within the professional scope of the Neopagan priest/ess. One of the primary reasons multiple relationships becomes such an ethical issue is the Neopagan community tends to be small and thus we often engage with each other in a variety of ways, making outright avoidance of multiple relationships a challenge.

Multiple relationships are not ethical problems in and of themselves—most of us in our everyday life negotiate a wide range of multiple relationships. For example, we may be friends with co-workers. We may have children and serve on the PTA and thus engage with teachers both as parents and as individuals concerned with the overall functioning of the school. Further if you live in a small or rural community, chances are high that engaging with others in diverse roles are part of your everyday life. What then makes a multiple relationship a problem? When they risk becoming harmful or exploitive.

Sonne[1] suggests several issues are central to determining the risk of harmful multiple relationships (we'll be discussing these in-depth throughout this section): (a) the degree to which individuals understand the professional parameters of the relationship; (b) the difference in power between the professional and the individual; (c) how long the professional relationship is slated to last; and (d) community setting of the relationship. When Sonne refers to the degree individuals understand professional parameters, this refers to how well you as a

Neopagan clergy person communicates your roles and responsibilities to your members. When members know what to expect, it makes it much less likely that you will engage in harmful behaviors that could violate the rights of your members—the process of knowing what to expect and agreeing to the parameters of the relationship is known as **Consent**. Within the counseling and the medical setting, a higher standard of consent is held and known as **Informed Consent**. Informed consent refers to the act of *fully* informing clients of what to expect within the counseling process and relationship. Specifically, the therapist delimits the scope of the relationship, the treatment methods and expected outcomes, and often fee schedule. In turn clients can then choose to agree to these conditions or withdraw from treatment. Agreement is typically demonstrated by signing a legal document re-iterating the parameters of the relationship; once this is signed it reinforces the fiduciary relationship between therapist and client—meaning the therapist is legally bound to be faithful, trustworthy, and to maintain the parameters of the consent.

Within the Neopagan ministry consent should be seen as an essential part of your work and it should look for a higher degree of informed consent. This means that all members are provided with the same information of the professional parameters of your work and responsibility to them. Unless you are engaging in a counseling setting, you can typically provide a handout to all members within a welcoming package that includes a line that states something to the effect of *by participating at [name of organization], you agree to the terms identified in this brochure*. If you engage in pastoral counseling, you will need to have each person you counsel sign a written informed consent detailing what to expect in the counseling process. What is included in an informed consent within the Neopagan ministry context?

>**Mission Statement:** A brief statement that describes the underlying purpose and values of the group. For example, *Here at [name of group] our purpose is to honor the Lord and Lady through shared worship and a nature-centered lifestyle.* This should be the central tenant that ALL members, clergy and laity are expected to uphold. Optionally, you can also delineate the core ethics and values of your organization.
>
>**Membership Benefits.** These are concise, but sufficiently detailed explanation of what benefits members can hope to gain by being a member of the group. It should explore how members may be emotionally and spiritually changed. It should be realistic and clear. Further, if you teach students for initiation and/or ordination, this should be disclosed here.
>
>**Membership Risks:** If you are operating a small coven where individuals

develop more personal and intimate relationships, you must disclose this environment and the potential social risks (such as confidentiality issues). If you work skyclad or engage in other ritual actions that may not be widely accepted within outside society or may prove anxiety provoking for prospective members this must be disclosed. Your risks and benefits statements should be specific to allow members to fully *understand* and *agree*. The key with risks is to imagine a wide range of possible negative reactions to what you do. For example, you might consider someone coming from an abuse background and you operate a skyclad worship service—a failure to disclose this at the outset (including a statement that states clothing optional) may lead to harm of this individual. This in turn places you at legal liability if it was not fully disclosed.

Procedural Requirements: This includes information about when meetings occur and what, if any, specific and uniform requirements there are for attending. This may also include a statement of time commitments, if individuals are expected to participate outside regularly scheduled meetings. This also includes outlining any educational requirements if you operate from an initiation (degree-program) structure. The steps for initiation and/or ordination should be clearly outlined and defined.

Minister Responsibility: It is a very good idea to delineate your responsibilities as a clergy—what you do for the members. This includes officiating community rituals, pastoral counseling (if applicable and sufficiently trained), teaching, and officiating private ceremonies (marriage/unions, birth, death) for example.

Confidentiality: Neopaganism firmly values confidentiality, as such prospective members should be informed about the parameters of confidentiality (what is protected and what is disclosed, e.g. harm to self or others, child or elder abuse). A word on **secrecy**: secrecy is *not* confidentiality. Confidentiality protects the participants (their names, identifying characteristics, personal information), while secrecy is associated with the degree of disclosure of a tradition's material and rituals. Secrecy can be problematic and can foster a sense of distrust and suspicion among participants—they may feel less secure about their experiences and the safety of tradition. Secrecy often reinforces unhealthy power dynamics and may inhibit individuals from asking necessary questions to make *informed decisions* about the degree they wish to commit to the tradition. Further, participants may raise suspicion and experience greater social discomfort if they are unable to disclose to friends and family what they are learning and working with. This then contributes to facilitating public distortions of Neopagan paths. I would generally recommend you avoid this component of your work and instead utilize a statement of copyright if you are distributing your own work and fearful of its cooption by other groups.

Fee Agreements: If you accept or charge fees—you need to be very clear about how much is collected, the purpose of fees and how they are utilized, and issues of refund/returns. Further if you obtain a 501(c)3 tax exemption status, this should be disclosed on all documents. This also means you will need a board of governors so to speak. This is a group of religious members who oversee your business functioning to ensure that monies are directed to the benefit of organization. Further, when organized as a business, members should be provided with information on filing complaints within the organization: who do they turn to if there is an issue?. Finally, most religious organizations establish a means to accept donations—individuals should be informed what are required fees and what are donation-based and thus optional.

Revoking Membership: Members need to know that they can leave the organization at any time for any reason without consequence. This also means that if you accept fees, you will need to disclose how monies are dealt with in the event a member leaves, for example returned or nonrefundable needs to be disclosed. Further members should be made aware at the beginning of their group participation under what circumstances may their membership be revoked. Finally, the informed consent should also note that members will never be threatened or coerced or retaliated against for leaving.

Liability Statement: These are statements releasing you and your organization from liability for negative experiences individuals may have as a member. It's important that your liability statements are developed in conjunction with a lawyer if you are operating a formal ministry.

Nondiscrimination Statement: It's always a good idea to emphasize your organization does not discriminate on the part of age, religion[2], race, ethnicity, gender, sexual orientation, class, and disability. This not only encourages the practice of openness and nondiscrimination, but also ensures that members adhere to this policy as well.

Informed consent goes a long way to ensuring that the relationship between you and your members remains professional—regardless of other types of relationships that may emerge based on necessity. Research has shown that professionals who utilize informed consent are less likely to engage in ethically harmful behavior. The primary reason for this is because the expectations for the relationships between you and your members are clearly defined: members know what to expect from you and their interaction in the environment. There is little ad-libbing so to speak. It also means that you have spent a fair amount of time delineating what type of environment you wish to create for your members and what your responsibilities are to them.

The next issue Sonne addresses is the difference in power between individuals and the one in charge. What this specifically means is the greater the difference, in other words the Neopagan priest/ess who holds a high degree of power *over* members, the greater the risk for entering into unethical multiple relationships. Clearly, a priest or priestess has greater power in most Neopagan religious structures because they often have greater education and the authority to admit (initiate) or deny members' access to greater authority. This means the priest/ess must be cautious if they require their members to engage with them in ways that are outside the parameters of clergy/member relationship (such as a sexual relationship for example). Again this can be countered through a uniform informed consent and self-monitoring that all members are treated equally and fairly. Further, having a system whereby individuals are invited to provide their opinion about how they would like to see the group operate can be another way of reducing the power differentials and the risk of taking advantage of members.

The third issue Sonne identifies is duration. The longer a group is together the more likely multiple relationships will emerge and become a problem. Short-run groups rarely form the intimate and patterned emotional interactions that long-term groups do. Thus a group that comes together only 8 times a year for Sabbats is unlikely to experience profound bonding and thus multiple relationships are unlikely to create significant challenges. This is related to the next element in Sonne.

The final aspect Sonne addresses is the issue of location, which translates to size. The risks associated with multiple relationships increases in smaller communities. As noted in the beginning of the section, this is one of the central challenges Neopagan clergy will face simply because most Neopagan communities are inherently small. A small group that meets weekly is much more vulnerable to the effects of multiple relationships impacting the group dynamics. The longer the group has been together and the smaller the group is, the higher the risk for a negative outcome for a multiple relationship. Clergy often meet their friends and even significant others from these small environments, as such extra care should be maintained when you are considering entering into a multiple relationships.

How then should one evaluate multiple relationships? Younggren and Gottlieb[3] suggest evaluating the potential relationship along five questions:

> "Is entering into a relationship in addition to the professional one necessary, or should I avoid it?" If you work within a small Neopagan community, chances are high that you may need multiple relationships for your own well-being. It is unrealistic for you to live as a hermit within your religious community. Further, the smallness of the community makes it likely that you will engage with members outside the minister–member role as they may work with you or work in locales you frequent or be related to other members in your family etc. In this fashion, it is critical to be able to assess your environment honestly. Avoiding multiple relationships should be the priority unless impossible or benefits the members.

> "Can the dual relationship potentially cause harm to [individual]?" It is critical to assess the multiple relationship from the perspective of harm. For example, if you become romantically involved with a member of your community, not only is this individual attached to you romantically and emotionally, but they depend on you and the community for their own social supports. If the relationship ends, you remain a member of the community, but this individual will likely have to leave. In this capacity, you are engaging in harm of a member of your community.

> "If harm seems unlikely or avoidable, would the additional relationship prove beneficial?" Not all multiple relationships are harmful, while harm can also be avoided based on action. Some multiple relationships can be helpful. For example, you may work as a clergy and as a teacher in your local community. A member's child may attend your class—not only will you understand the child's religious commitments, but you may also serve to provide a certain degree of protection for that child's religious differences.

> "Is there a risk that the dual relationship [another term for multiple relationships] could disrupt the [religious] relationship?" Your primary responsibility is your clergy role and your responsibility to your laity. The de-

gree of disruption (potential and actual) of your capacity to carry out this role or your community's capacity to maintain their religious affiliation and comfort within the group should always be weighed when considering multiple relationships. If disruption cannot be ameliorated, than the multiple relationship should be avoided.

"Can I evaluate this matter objectively?" Most of the time we are somewhat blind to our own needs and abilities. We often think we are more likely to handle a situation better than we actually do. It is always a good idea to have another clergy member to speak with about the situation. Networking with other clergy in your faith or remaining in contact with individuals you have previously studied with to get feedback is important. Just remember never to use identifying characteristics or names if you are having an issue with a specific member of your laity.

A Word on Sex

Sex within the Neopagan clergy context needs to be discussed in two ways: sex that occurs with a member in the context of a romantic relationship (a multiple relationship) and sex utilized within ritual. Because the Neopagan religious community is often small and isolated in geographical areas, if you as the priest/ess are not in a committed romantic relationship prior to beginning your group it is possible that you will meet someone in the group whom you are attracted to. Because a romantic relationship with a member of the group can create harm, not only to that individual should the relationship fall apart, but also to the group as a whole (particularly if the group is small; larger groups are more buffered from these effects), you should not enter into this relationship unless both of you are fully aware of the potential consequences and have discussed how you will address them. If your partner is also your co-clergy person *before* you work together, you should both take a substantial period of time to discuss how you will work together while the relationship is positive and should it become harmful. Just because you are romantically involved does not mean you will work professionally well together—and problems with the clergy will harm the members.

Sex within the ritual setting.... I **_strongly_** suggest you avoid incorporating sacred sex within your religious environment for several reasons:

> A large portion of the population, both men and women, have been sexually abused as children—for many this is an unresolved and unhealed issue. Individuals who have been victimized are more likely to be sexually victimized again. They often feel they cannot say no to figures

in authority and may feel coerced into engaging in sex because it is presented as "sacred", "good for them", "having it in the religious setting will help them heal" etc. In this fashion, pairing sex with religion often acts as a form of coercion, regardless of its theological justifications or even the use of informed consent—particularly if it is between the religious leader and the members or the member is required to watch. In this fashion remember, you will never know the whole mental health and social history of your members. You **must** assume that at least one member has been abused or has mental health issues, whereby religious-justified sex within the group is likely to create harm.

Sex within the religious setting exponentially increases the harm to other members, the risk of religious indoctrination, and disempowerment of members; largely because this increases the power differentials.

It increases your legal risks—consent does not protect against sexual coercion. Even if members agree to have sex within the context, this does not mean they were not coerced and sexually assaulted in the court of law.

Most individuals feel sexual intimacy is a private experience—public displays can cause anxiety and distress—thus creating harm. Further, individuals often hold very strong opinions about sexual orientation, which can create substantial conflict and even physical harm within a group.

Sexual relationships within the context of a religious experience is a multiple relationship—as such it must be assumed to cause harm before it can be assumed to bring benefit. Remember, even if only one individual perceives harm in the group—it constitutes an ethical violation.

If you feel the need to include sex within your religious experience, I strongly encourage you to consider what needs this serves for you and to evaluate your own sexual practices, needs, and sources of arousal. Additionally, if you have been sexually abused as a child and feel the need to include sexual experience within your religious setting, it is critical that you seek professional counseling regarding your experience to ensure that you are developing a healthy, safe, and satisfying sexual behaviors. A role as the clergy cannot be utilized as a means to heal one's past.

8
Ethical Issues & Money

There are three perspectives within Neopagan paths in terms of money: (a) accepting fees from members for the duration of their attachment to the group and learning process; (b) accepting no fee at all; and (c) sharing material responsibilities between all members. Each of these choices has ethical implications that deserve some elucidation. Further the exchange of money also has legal implications that need to be discussed.

Accepting Fees

Accepting fees has become an increasingly common practice within many Neopagan groups. Fees can vary substantially in terms of monthly and yearly cost. For example, many online Neopagan groups who train and initiate individuals charge monthly fees ranging from $15 to $30 per month. The underlying rationale is that such fees serve to support administrative, lesson production, and web hosting costs. Many large Neopagan training groups tend to operate their religious structure with a firmly developed business model that has an underlying goal of selling a specific service or commodity to individuals, which can conflict with the underlying ethics of a religious practice. Often these groups may be substantially larger than a traditional face-to-face group, with limited access to or contact with trained priests and priestesses, spiritual mentors, and the High Priest or High Priestess. This can raise the ethical issue of money becoming the primary motivation and the business model of fee-for-service becoming the underlying source of ethics. The challenge raised by this is the business model does not necessarily coincide with the ethical charges associated with the professional role of Priest/ess and High Priest/ess. This does not mean that accepting fees is itself a problem, rather if you elect this model there are a few things you need to consider:

Legally, if you accept a tax-exempt status you will need to be meticulous in your monitoring of how you accept fees and how you use your fees. Further, accepting fees increases your legal fiduciary responsibility to your students. You must make good on the claims you advertise to students. Accepting fees often places you at higher risk of lawsuits and complaints associated with organizations such as the Better Business Bureau. Largely because individuals paying for a service often hold certain expectations about how they feel they should be individually treated, whether this is realistic or not. If you fail to live up to these expectations, you run the risk of individuals seeking legal action and compensation. You need to be very explicit in your disclosure of how fees are used and whether there is a refund policy and under what conditions coupled with what individuals will obtain with their payment (what products, so to speak, are they purchasing).

Ethically, you will need to ensure that accepting money does not undermine your capacity to be an engaged spiritual mentor, whose is primarily in charge of maintaining the quality of the teaching and ritual environment. If accepting fees is linked to a higher number of students due to relying on this as your primary source of income, it is highly likely that the integrity of your teaching and leadership skills will be undermined to some degree. Again, if you will not be directly involved in your student's learning and spiritual development, this needs to be fully disclosed on the agreement/payment forms (informed consent). Prospective students need to know who they will be communicating with and how they will be learning. Well designed programs generally utilize older students as mentors—these students ideally have sufficient knowledge to foster new students learning and growth. This is one way to have a large group without completely losing site of a sense of religious community and connection.

It's important that your understanding of accepting fees is consistent with and grounded within your theo/alogical charge. Everything you do as a priest/ess or High Priest/ess should be deeply situated within the spiritual ethics and beliefs of your tradition. Money (or another form of trade) has been a part of religious life since religious leadership became a profession within the community, beginning with the first shamans. Traditionally providing coinage or other trade items was largely related to a specific service offered by the religious leader, such as healing or divination. Additionally, large state-supported religions often collected fees from adherents, which went to supporting government processes. Finally, as religions became increasingly separate from supporting government functions, donations were about supporting a larger professional clergy as well as the larger overarching organization of the faith. The rationale of money exchange for healing, teaching, or divination services related to the notion that it demonstrated a respect for the skills of the individual on the part of the prospective client and promoted reciprocity. The rationale for donations to fund the professional office for the clergy or the larger religious group was often seen as a requirement for devotees to show their appreciation for and devotion to the Divine, Whose presence was seen as embodied by the Priest/ess. Knowing what theo/alogical expectations are fulfilled by payment can serve to not only help you set up the right energy for fee collection, but also ensure that the fees are utilized appropriately.

As a religious leader, you also need to ensure that your tradition and faith remains accessible to individuals regardless of their capacity to pay. This means one of the following options: (a) create a fund to support individuals who meet the financial need requirements; (b) utilizing a sliding scale set up based on income levels (students with higher incomes pay a larger tuition fee); or (b) use a suggested donation option, where students are given options for how much they can realistically donate. However you set your fee schedule, the guidelines for exemptions or reductions should be clear and consistently applied to all members.

Ideally, fees should enhance your tradition and the services you are able to offer. If you accept fees they should be able to increase the quality and types of services you offer your members. Members are more likely to pay fees (particularly monthly or high yearly fees) if they see direct benefits to them.

Not Charging

Many Neopagan groups still operate without charging fees. Priests/esses and High Priest/esses donate their time, energy, and knowledge to fostering the spiritual development of their members. Specifically, smaller traditions that are restricted to face-to-face environment are often more likely to reject charging.

For example, Ellen Cannon Reed writes the following:

> ...the teaching we do, is also a gift to the Gods and Goddesses. We do not charge for it. Doing so would negate our gift....
>
> If we accepted money for our teaching, we would, in effect, become employees of our students. Students would be relieved of any responsibility to work, grow, study, learn, or even attend classes. It would be impossible for a teacher to train under those conditions.[1]

Reed holds that accepting of money for one's work as priest or priestess undermines the primary theological charge of the office—that is dedicating oneself in service to the Divine. As such it is one's duty to pass on this information and teach as a visible way in which one may demonstrate their dedication to the Divine. Within this perspective, accepting money is unethical because it violates the primary relationship between the priest/ess and the Divine. Additionally, Reed suggests that accepting money undermines the authority of the priest/ess in relation to the students. This is consistent with the power structure that Reed adheres to within her own interpretation of Wicca as a small, tradition-based initiatory path with very strict boundaries between members and clergy. In this fashion, Reed's interpretation of accepting money is seen as undermining a divinely inspired metaethic, coupled with undermining an important power–over structural relationship. While I personally adhere to a no-fee requirement for similar theo/alogical reasons as Cannon; not accepting fees does not necessarily create a clear distinction between student and teacher. As we discussed in a previous chapter, the boundaries between member and priest/ess are established by how the priest/ess chooses to interact with his or her members—both accepting or not accepting fees can support hierarchical nor equitable structures, which I do not adhere to. However, Reed is correct it noting that a relationship between fees and degree of work for students. For some students a no-fee arrangement may lead to less interest and commitment as students do not risk losing material gain if they are not working; while other students may feel a greater sense of responsibility for their learning if they are not charged.

Shared Material Responsibility

Another popular method of "funding" your religious community is distributive in nature—that is having all members contribute materially to the community by providing items needed. This is often very popular in structures that are highly egalitarian that seek to reduce the divisions between clergy and membership. Having members bring items to meetings also increases their own sense of commitment and builds a sense of contributing to the whole. This can be an important balancing point if you do not accept fees. Many individuals often feel the need to give something back (reciprocity) when they are receiving services for free. In this fashion, allowing students to bring ritual items, foodstuffs, and other items for the group can be an emotionally rewarding process for the students, benefit the group, and can also serve as a learning experience as members learn to shop for or craft certain ritual items. Shared responsibility often supports the theological view of what you give, returns to you.

There are a few challenges with this method. First, the priest/ess should ensure that no one member should become the primary source of material, thus increasing a risk of that person developing an unhealthy sense of responsibility that places them at risk of being taken advantage of by the group. Second, the priest/ess needs to ensure that competition between members over the quality of items brought and their cost does not emerge. Third, some members simply do not have substantial income to be able to participate in bringing items but may feel embarrassed, pressured, or ashamed about this and thus may quietly struggle, placing themselves emotionally and financially at risk to keep up with the "Jonses" so to speak. Finally, there is the question of how to hold individuals accountable for the material they are slated to bring and how to ensure that necessary ritual material is always present in case someone "forgets". If individuals become penalized for failing to bring material to their religious service, this can raise some ethical issues about the reliance upon materiality versus spirit and lead to a significant misdirection away from the divine and into materialism. These situations, however, can be beneficially used to test the creativity of the priest/ess to lead rituals without material items—something each should be able to do.

❧

Financial issues will become a part of every priest/esses life who works professionally and as such should not be addressed when a crisis hits. It's important to enter into the professional role with a good idea of what is necessary financially for you to maintain this role. Further complicating factors is many priests and priestesses have issues around money. This can include such issues as:

- Being paid for services rendered (do I deserve this?);

- Being realistic about how much money is necessary to manage a ministry (do I have a good business plan? How do I budget? What material items are necessary? What are my operating costs?);

- Having a theological and ethical framework in place for how to deal with money (what does my faith say about money?);

- How much time do I want to be committed to my work? (if you do not plan to spend a lot of time with your students or members, do not accept fees); and

- How do I feel about money in general and how well do I manage it in my personal life.

These are important questions to begin to ask yourself when you are exploring the "business" of ministry. And it's especially important that you spend time considering how you feel about money personally and how you manage it in your own life. How we spend money in our personal lives will often be mirrored in how we use it in our professional ones. So if you are an impulsive buyer personally, there's a high chance you will do this with professional money and as such, money may not be an option for your ministry or you may need to higher someone to manage it. Additionally, if you have a high-degree of anxiety around money, perhaps you never had enough as a child, perhaps you grew up with materially-focused parents, or you and your partner fight about money, then money will evoke emotional issues for you. These should be addressed *before* you begin to accept money.

9
Working with Children & Adolescents

An Overview of Development

One of the most important issues to remember when working with children (aged <12) and adolescents (legally aged 13–17) is that neurobiological development is not completed until between the ages of 21 and 24, with women before men reaching full development first. In other words, the human brain is not fully "adult" until well after the age of adolescence is completed; specifically, the areas critical for a mature spiritual identity, the frontal lobes of the brain. The frontal lobes of the brain are associated with improved impulse control, planning and goal setting, organizing, refining emotional processing, cognition, moral development, empathy and perspective taking, and the development of personality. This is not to say that children and adolescents *lack* these skill areas, but rather they are areas that remain works in progress—which mean children and adolescents don't always get it right and they typically do not see the world the same way adults do, in other words children and adolescents are *not* mini-adults.

As we grow, the frontal lobes develop more dense neuronal connections, a process known as arborization (a result of learning whereby the more dense the connections the more resilient the brain and the more effective it processes information), coupled with a process known as myelination (this is the thin sheath that covers the neuronal networks, much like the rubber insulation of your electrical plugs and wires, that facilitates smooth and speedy electrical functioning). Human beings are the only species alive at this time with such a long period of development, which has the advantage of enabling our brains to grow exponentially and acquire the wide range of social–cultural and natural information we need to successfully negotiate our complex lives. The challenge, of course, is that with such a long period of development, children and adolescents are uniquely different from adults and they do not have consistent capabilities in their emotional and cognitive processing. Let's now take a look at some core issues about development in children and adolescents.

Developmental & the Spiritual Context

Birth–7

From birth to age 7, children make rapid changes in their motor, cognitive, and language areas. Depending on which developmental theorist you focus on (Piaget or Vygotsky), there is an emphasis that children manifest both their innate biological capabilities and are shaped by their surrounding social contexts. There are three specific developmental areas that are essential for children in this age group: (a) motor development; (b) cognitive development; and (c) social development. Motor development begins during the prenatal period and early infancy as a cluster of automatic reflexes; between 4 and 6 months of age infants begin to demonstrate increasing volitional (in their control) movements, such as sitting up, directing eye gaze, rudimentary babbling, and shaking of arms of legs. Between 6 and 9 months of age, most infants begin to crawl and demonstrate the capacity to direct their motor behavior toward small goals (interests) and to rapidly begin to explore their environment. By 12 months of age, most infants have learned to walk. At the age of 2, many children demonstrate more refined walking patterns and may also start to jump and engage in a variety of physical play. As physical behavior becomes increasingly more complex, this in turn helps strengthen not only motor areas of the brain, but also issues of planning and behavioral organization. This is known developmentally as the Piaget's *sensorimotor stage* (up to the age of 2). Motor activities are essential for young children.

In addition to motor development, children at this age also make rapid cognitive changes that are markedly related not only to their innate biology, but also to their environment. Piaget labeled the cognitive element of this stage as *preoperational*. During this cognitive stage, the child cannot perspective take, that is recognize that others feel and see the world different from the child. Piaget called this *egocentrism*, which you might remember from Chapter 5. Children make rapid changes in their language acquisition moving quickly from one-word communication to grammatically correct full sentences. Children intuitively understand that words represent internally generated ideas and objects and external objects. During this stage, children are innately curious about the world around them and have a capacity to rapidly acquire information about their world. Reading and talking to children is essential for healthy development of language.

Socially, children at this stage become increasingly aware of the social climate around them. They move from a firm attachment to one caregiver, often their mother, to their immediate family and to their peers. Children quickly recognize that language is a primary gateway for fostering social connections and readily begin talking to others—in fact infants as young as 6 months old will engage in "babble" with other infants when placed in day care. We begin to see certain social dispositions emerge, such as shyness or extroversion. Children are highly aware of their surrounding social contexts and will begin to adapt/assimilate information from these environments to their own behavior. In particularly, children begin modeling their behavior based on the adults around them. Adults can greatly aid children's social development by modeling healthy social behavior and encouraging healthy social interactions (sharing, for example). The innate social orientation also primes the child to acquire rapid information about their natural and cultural environments that will lay the foundation for their later adult survival.

Eric Erikson felt this age group moved through three specific psychosocial stages of development: trust versus mistrust (first year of life), autonomy versus shame and doubt (ages 1 to 3), and initiative versus guilt (ages 3 to 5). In the first year of life, Erikson felt the most important aspect of social development (that is how one sees him or herself in relation to the world) was the development of healthy attachment. Infants need to feel that their caregivers are consistent, reliable, and trustworthy. We learn our most basic concept of trust during this early stage of imprinting. Erikson felt that when infants grew up with unstable parents and experienced inconsistent or unpredictable responses to their emotional and physiological needs, they developed a sustained mistrust of the world around them. In this capacity children need consistent and reliable care whereby their basic emotional, cognitive, social, and physical needs are met. Children need to *feel* and *know* they are secure and loved. As the infant develops, they begin to explore the world around them. Erikson felt the development of walking unassisted was essential to a lifelong perception of one's autonomy—one's separate self. This also corresponds to the kind of egocentrism of thought that Piaget noted at this age. Children see themselves as the center of the world, because they have begun to miraculously experience themselves as separate from their caregivers. They can move on their own, achieve objects they desire, and can more effectively communicate what they want. When their fledging sense of autonomy (both expressed through motor independence and emotional/verbal communication) are contradicted inappropriately by adults, children can develop a profound sense of shame and doubt. Children need to be allowed to make mistakes and experience their own resiliency and children's self-expressions should be honored. This does not mean, however, that we do not correct the child when they engage in dangerous behavior—it means that we are aware that *how* we correct children can impact how they will come to trust their own judgment. Finally, Erikson felt that between the ages of 3 and 5, children begin to express their own drives and take the initiative. We see a marked increase in imaginative play and spontaneous game development. Children begin to step up and determine their own activities in the day and entertain themselves and each other. They seek out a wider range of peer interaction and can begin to take responsibility for small tasks. Erikson felt that children must be provided with opportunities to develop and engage in tasks and to achieve their small goals without being taught they are narcissistic or bad for wanting to engage in their own activities. Children need to have choices and be able to make age-appropriate decisions in order to develop healthy later-life goal-directed behavior. In short, the very traditional way of raising children to do as the parent dictates can undermine their capacity as adults to achieve their goals and create.

Developmental Spiritual Care Note

Once a child reaches the age of 2, do not expect them to be able to easily sit through any long religious ritual. Children require physical movement and often feel compelled to talk and be an integral part of the social environment—after all to them, and rightly so, the world revolves around them. Children biologically have very *short* attention spans and will tend to lose interest when they are ignored—that doesn't mean they won't observe adult behavior, however. As such, if you are working with families with young children, you will likely want to develop specific rituals for families with young children that incorporate tactile (touch), fun movement, storytelling with pictures preferably, and actively involve the children in talking. If you opt to remove children from their parents to attend a "Sunday School" so to speak, the same principles should follow. Most children can be engaged (providing it has a lot of internally shifting activities) for thirty minutes. Never expect children to sit for prolonged periods of time—kids fidget and their brains are craving movement and stimuli. Finally, with older young children, giving them choices and engaging them in the ritual development can go a long way to not only fostering their social and personal development, but will also ensure their attention and engagement.

Ages 7–12

Piaget labeled this age as the *concrete operational stage* and signifies rapid cognitive development—which we typically see associated with formal school training. Children show a capacity to understand more complex topics, although still tend to focus their attention on the literal. They are no longer ego-focused, but seek out peers to develop more permanent relationships. Often times during this stage, children develop the "best friend" relationship, which in turn helps them emotionally adjust to the school environment and transition away from their parents safely into this environment. Erikson felt that children during these ages were focused on developing **industry** and **identity.** Children begin to take active roles in their own development and begin to focus their attention for prolonged periods of time. Children often begin to express interests in specific activities, ranging from sports to artistic endeavors, and can demonstrate a high degree of commitment to these activities. Children also begin to manifest a capacity for work and self-monitoring. Children at this stage are also more aware of differences and begin to model parental/adult patterns of discrimination. This means that some children may begin to be ostracized and feel socially inferior if adults in authority do not model encouraging, accepting and tolerant behavior that supports fledging desires for achievement. As the child moves into early adolescence (around 10), Erikson felt that critical elements of one's sense of self began to form. In this fashion, children become aware of themselves in relation to their peers and will often begin to compare themselves against an idealized image of what they perceive to be normal and socially popular. Further, children in this stage tend to be less interested in spending time with their parents and may also begin to demonstrate mild opposition their parents' authority as they begin to clarify their own unique identity. This can lead to a wide range of emotional struggles for the developing child, particularly associated with self esteem.

Developmental Spiritual Care Note

Children in this age group have experience within structured environments and have developed a capacity for sustained focus in an activity. Children are also developing more complex cognitive abilities and are able to communicate clearly with adults at this stage. Further children also begin to understand basic concepts of morality and can also begin to understand basic elements of theology. More formal instruction on the elements of your faith can begin at this stage—keep in mind that children learn best in constructive educational environments whereby students co-create and discover knowledge together through activities that are imaginative, hands-on, exploratory, and diverse. In other words, lecturing just doesn't work for children in this age group—nor does an authoritative approach work (*Do as I say because I am the adult*)—again keeping in mind children need to be able to engage and direct their behavior and make choices for developmental purposes. Further, don't be surprised as children reach between the ages of 10 and 11, they may express more opposition and lack of interest or they may be preoccupied with issues associated with having a non-majority faith than most other children in their general peer group. As such, these issues should be addressed. Finally, children in this age group can be expected to participate in short rituals and handle responsibility for elements of a ritual. It can abe a fun activity to have children create their own ritual that puts together elements of what they are learning. They then can perform this ritual for their parents and elders in the faith.

Ages 13–18

We've entered adolescence. Most children by the time they reach 13 begin to demonstrate marked physiological changes, specifically the development of secondary sex characteristics (menstruation, breast development, vocal changes, increased interest in sex and romantic relationships, and growth [both height and weight]). This is a time of rapid hormonal changes and with that comes emotional upheaval. This also activates risk-taking behavior and we often find many adolescents, particularly boys, with poor impulse control—teens do what they feel in the moment. It is a time of substantial emphasis on social relationships and often a great deal of pressure to achieve and identify career goals and aspirations. Teens experience life in vivid emotional color. It is a time of experimentation with a wide range of possible social identities and roles. Teens may fluctuate dramatically in their personal interests and this often includes religious exploration. The key with teens is to recognize the parameters of what is normal, healthy exploration and what suggests the development of a problem: lack of self-care (too thin, not eating, not bathing, gaining excessive weight); persisting negative self talk (makes frequent disparaging statements about themselves); sudden drop in school performance; sudden change in social affiliation/friendships; isolation and excessive sleeping; frequent or persisting patterns of anger or despair; frequent nonspecific physical complaints (particularly gastrointestinal problems); engaging in risky or dangerous behavior. These are warning signs that there are potentially serious psychological issues developing and interventions should be made to assess the risks for the teen.

Developmental Spiritual Care Note

Young teens benefit from a positive social and religious experience that fosters positive peer relationships and a healthy self-esteem. Honoring the transition from childhood to adolescence is a positive way of helping teens make sense of their changing bodies and emotional outlooks. Further utilizing the rich mythic and theological heritage of Neopagan traditions to help young men and women develop a positive gender identity that is both empowered and balanced can be critical in helping the teens to cope with the challenges of adolescence. Teens are able to fully participate in ritual life and older teens, depending on the degree of parental support and involvement, may be able to initiate into a tradition. Finally, allow teens to make choices within their religious experiences is critical to fostering a bond with teens and also ensuring their healthy development.

Ethics & Legal Issues

We've talked at length about the developmental issues raised by children and teens; however one area that is critical is how to incorporate teens and children into your religious community in an ethical and legally protective way. Because Neopagan traditions are not yet mainstream and widely accepted religious faiths, teens may seek you out *without* parental support or knowledge. It is critical to remember that in most countries, and in the United States in general, individuals under the age of 18 are *not* considered legally independent individuals. That means, parental consent, with the exception of some medical issues, is required to ensure your own legal protection. Further, teens who come to your group without parental consent often lack the necessary social supports to become fully engaged in the faith and to gain the full benefits of its practice. In this fashion, it is generally recommend that you do not accept members under the age of 18 without parental consent. Further, I would recommend you confine your acceptance to older teens should you accept them into your group. Another important point regarding teens: teens also have a tendency to develop strong feelings toward individuals, so be cautious that your teens are protected from developing romantic inclinations with adults in the group and ensure that other adults in the group respect the social boundaries between them and their younger members. If you opt to avoid the challenges raised by incorporating teens into your group when their families are not members, consider having a book list and web sites for the serious adolescent to explore and invite them to return when they are 18 or older and really feel called to this faith after taking time to learn about it.

Ethically speaking, providing age-appropriate activities to foster spiritual development is critical. In this fashion, your religious interventions and teaching methods need to match the specific psychosocial needs of your young members. Expecting a five year old to demonstrate perfect judgment and self-control is unrealistic given their natural tendencies at this age. Further, expecting this young person to be able to understand the concept of immanence would be unrealistic. When we develop inappropriate developmental interventions we can harm the child by setting them up for failure and experiencing negative social feedback (often times adults start yelling when the child doesn't do what the adult expects is normal). Again, children and teens are *not* adults and they do not see the world with the same social parameters as adults do. *They lack much of the self control that adults have.* Thus in keeping with the ethics of do no harm, it's important that if you have young members of your tradition that you develop religious interventions that are age appropriate and are conscious of fostering the intellectual, physical, and socioemotional needs of your young members. This can further model for parents the appropriate ways of relating to children and can reduce in-the-family conflict due to a mismatch between a child's natural developmental impulses and misunderstandings adults might have about what is "normal".

Confidentiality is another area that can emerge within the context of young persons, particularly adolescents. Generally speaking, if a parent wants to know what is happening you must inform them. You do not have the same privileges that physicians and psychologists and other counselors (in *some* circumstances) that ensures that you keep the privacy of your young member. While there is some debate that teens over the age of 16 should be permitted to have full confidential agreements on par with adults, it is generally an ethically appropriate idea to inform your young persons that what they tell you may not be kept from their parents and that you may be legally required to talk with them. Use these situations as an opportunity to help your young person talk with their parents—teens do better when they have open and honest communication with their parents. I generally encourage young priest and priestess to use their authority to help parents and children communicate and to help parents listen to their teens, even when the issues are challenging and uncomfortable (sex, pregnancy, substance abuse, and mental health issues for example). When you present yourself as a reliable and supportive individual who remains calm and empathetic in the face of difficult issues, you can go a long way to help the young person talk with their parents. Further, modeling empathy and calm to parents can also help them better communicate with their adolescent.

If you have young persons in your group, there are certain ritual elements that are definitely off-limits: skyclad, scourging[1] and any sexual behavior. All three of these would be considered placing the young person at risk and would generally be classified as child endangerment, sex abuse, or physical abuse depending on the behavior engaged in and will prosecuted under the law accordingly. Further, they are simply not appropriate for a developing child and teen who are still trying to learn their boundaries and to establish a positive physical identity and comfort.

Reflecting on Developmental Issues

Activity 1: Your Own Developmental Timeline

One of the best activities to engage with before you begin working with children is to reflect upon your own development. We often hear the phrase, "remember what we were like when we were younger?" as a hope that we will apply our own shared experience coping with developmental issues when we encounter children. However, most of the time, we act as the dreaded "adults". The reason is adults have their own developmental issues that they have to work through and on and that often takes precedence over where they were when children; add to this our cultures often teach us how to be an adult (and we in turn pass this on to our children). Nevertheless, the healthiest adult is one who does relate to the child's developmental experiences and can take a facilitative role, rather than a dictatorial one. This is the difference between the adult who encourages a child but sets firm boundaries to prevent harm and the adult who simply says "no" and "don't" and "do it my way." We can go a long way to becoming the former and stilling the latter impulse by actively reflecting on our own experiences. This can be done through a journal (or creative project) of creating our own timeline—feel free to pull out all the photo albums of yourself if you have any. Draw out a timeline of your childhood and adolescence and write about your memories and your experiences. Be sure to include adults that you felt encouraged you and instances where you had conflict. Review both of these types of experiences and determine if there were developmental issues that the adults were ignoring or struggling to cope with. Consider how you might have altered the situation as an adult now and someone who knows a little bit more about development.

Activity 2: Childhood Religious Experiences

In your journal, take time to write about your experiences in your religion as a child and adolescent. What do you remember as your response to the religion? Were their moments when you felt inspired and connected, or bored and disconnected? How did adults around you treat you? What kinds of involvement did you have in ritual life or learning the beliefs of the religion? How were you instructed? Reflecting on what you know about development and spiritual care, what might you have done differently?

Activity 3: Develop Developmentally Appropriate Lessons

Here's your theological goal: teach the concept that Nature is sacred. Now taking your journal, brainstorm three activities for individuals in the above three age groups. Identify the length of time for the lesson, any materials utilized, and if you are writing a ritual be specific. Review your work and consider discussing it with friends to assess whether it would be developmentally achievable for each group. Is it realistic or too challenging?

10
When to Refer

One of the most important skills you can develop as a professional priest/ess working in service of your members is your capacity to know your limitations. We all have limitations both personal and professional that we must learn and work within. Often times work limitations are delineated in your job description or determined by legal guidelines; however for Neopagan clergy there is often times no over-arching guidelines and due to separation of church and state, there are often ambiguous legal boundaries. As such, it becomes critically important for Neopagan clergy to carefully define their professional boundaries long before they actually begin to work with members. And it is also important that each clergy takes the time to learn how state/country laws have been applied to other clerics in other faiths to ensure that you are practicing within the appropriate boundaries of the law. We'll be talking in greater depth in the last chapter of this text about establishing professional boundaries when we examine how to establish a Code of Ethics. In this chapter, our attention will be focused on knowing personal limitations and exploring two broad areas when referring to external helping resources is important.

Personal Limitations

We often think of limitations as a mark against us. We strive in our day-to-day lives to seem impermeable and perfect. Oftentimes, our desire to be faultless blinds us to our very real and necessary imperfections. Striving toward perfection and being blind to one's faults often comes from very real ego needs that mask underlying feelings of doubt, shame, and guilt. Often times individuals who strive toward perfection and never acknowledge their faults or mistakes have learned to equate limitations with profound weakness and powerlessness.

To acknowledge one's limitations means to have lost power—and this often comes from challenging experiences in childhood where mistakes were ridiculed or even harshly punished.

On the other end of the spectrum, some clergy have been wounded in their pasts that they cannot accept the skills they have and do well with. Low self-esteem, shame, and guilt may prevent individuals from acknowledging and utilizing all their skills in service to others and the Neopagan faiths. This, too, presents a distortion of our abilities—the denial of all of one's strengths and positive contributions to a situation. This in turn can limit personal growth and also the degree to which you involve yourself in your member's lives. You may be someone who restricts the role of clergy to only an area you feel firmly perfect in, such as ritual conducting, but limit all deeper contact with members because you feel shame, embarrassment, or harbor feelings that you are a bad person and incapable.

Whether you hold beliefs that imperfections make you a bad or less-than person or if you hold beliefs that you are so flawed you cannot do *anything* right, both of these reflect a distortion on what your actual limitations and abilities are. In one, you may take on too much responsibility; in the latter you may significantly limit your contributions to the world around you. Both of these wounded positions need healing and this healing ideally should take place *prior* to becoming a clergy. And the healing process, whether engaged in with another clergy or with a professional counselor, is not only healing but educational. They provide you with a lived experience of how to work with individuals during specific forms of emotional and personal crisis. You have experience to draw from both to professionally model and to increase your capacity to empathize with your members. At the same time, by acknowledging your own woundings and imperfections, you open yourself up to a new kind of relationship with others that is more authentic and whole. I've often encouraged clergy and clients alike to recognize that our imperfections allow others to take center stage and remind us that we are part of a community, not solitary saviors. Our struggles allow others to actively participate in our lives—if we do all things perfect, then those around us will struggle to find their place in our lives; they will struggle to find ways to participate and reciprocate.

Knowing when to say when, not only allows you to form authentic relationships with others, but also ensures those entrusted to your service receive optimal care. When you know your limits, you won't be trying to fix a challenge that is over your head and thus risk making it worse. This might emerge when faced with medical or psychiatric challenges—potentially delaying important care and treatment. Additionally, knowing our limitations and respecting them not only allows us to grow and learn in new areas, but also to avoid taking on a paternalistic attitude toward those we work in service to. If we feel we are perfect and without faults or limits, then we often demand those we work with to do as we say, rather than empower them to find their own solutions. We also do a profound disservice by presenting the illusion that perfection is possible. It's not. There will always be someone who knows a little bit more than you or does something a little bit better or different in a field you consider yourself an expert in. It doesn't mean they are perfect, it just means they've had more opportunities for learning.

There is a wide range of ways to assess your limits. In the following activity, you'll have an opportunity to journal about your strengths and your limitations. To make the most of your self-assessment it's important to be honest and specific. While it can be tempting to rush through the activity, you'll lose out on important opportunities for self-discovery. Additionally, recognize that the activity to follow is not a one-time process. We are not stagnant, but always changing, as such our limitations change and sometimes substantially. Additionally being able to honestly and realistically assess ourselves, we can make conscious choices for learning. For example, thirteen years ago I worked as a Crisis Hotline operator—my training was working with individuals who were suicidal. I was comfortable with handling these immediate situations, but when I started getting calls from an individual with significant paranoia and persisting mental health challenges that did not fall under the "crisis" label, I realized I was out of my depth and needed to refer the caller to a local mental health clinic. At the same time, this event sparked my desire to obtain more training and education to expand my skills and reduce my limitations in this area. In this fashion, our limits can guide us toward new areas of growth and this should be embraced and welcomed as it ultimately means we are never a "finished" product and that we can continue to live a vibrant life full of learning and forming new relationships and having even more types of gifts to give to others.

Assessing Your Limits Activity

Over the next four pages are worksheets for you to complete. On each you will see three circles, the center circle is you. In this center circle jot down all the skills you have that you do well according to the topic noted at the top (Work-related Skills; Educational; Skills; Relational Skills; Neopagan/Clergy skills); skills you would label yourself an "expert" at. Don't limit yourself to any "traditional" résumé-like skills either—think out of the box and recognize there may be some overlap between the categories, so it is perfectly acceptable to put a skill more than once. The key is to be honest and put the skills you are strong in at the center of the circle. If you do not have anything listed, than you need to consider whether you're short-changing yourself with low self-esteem.

As the spheres extend outward, write skills that you have but that are less well-developed. By the time you get to the outermost space around the last sphere, you should have skills you *cannot* do at this time. To help you better identify missing skills, consider your friends and family and how they help you through situations. If you do not have skills listed in any of the outermost spheres than you need to look at why you may be fearful of acknowledging your imperfections—we all have lots of skills missing.

Once you've completed your spherework, take time to review them. Consider the following questions:

- In what ways might the strengths in all my spheres foster my clergy role?

- Are there any strengths that might inhibit my clergy role that might need to be tempered?

- What broad areas do I struggle with the most (work, relational, educational, and clerical) and what are the factors that have impacted the development of this area?

- What are some strategies I could do to strengthen one of the weaker areas? Can I realistically do this?

- What are my "weakest" skills and how might they be improved?

- Who do I know that manifests the skills I have that are less developed and how do they exhibit this skill? How did they develop it? What can I learn from them?

Take time to journal about what you've written to expand upon it. You might wish to consider what aspects of your life shaped your skills. What role your family played, your social and cultural opportunities and influences, and other elements of your life that have encouraged, discouraged, denied, or prohibited different skills.

Specific Situational Limitations

Knowing your personal limitations is half the battle of becoming a successful clergy, the second part of the battle is knowing what to do with your limitations

Work Skills

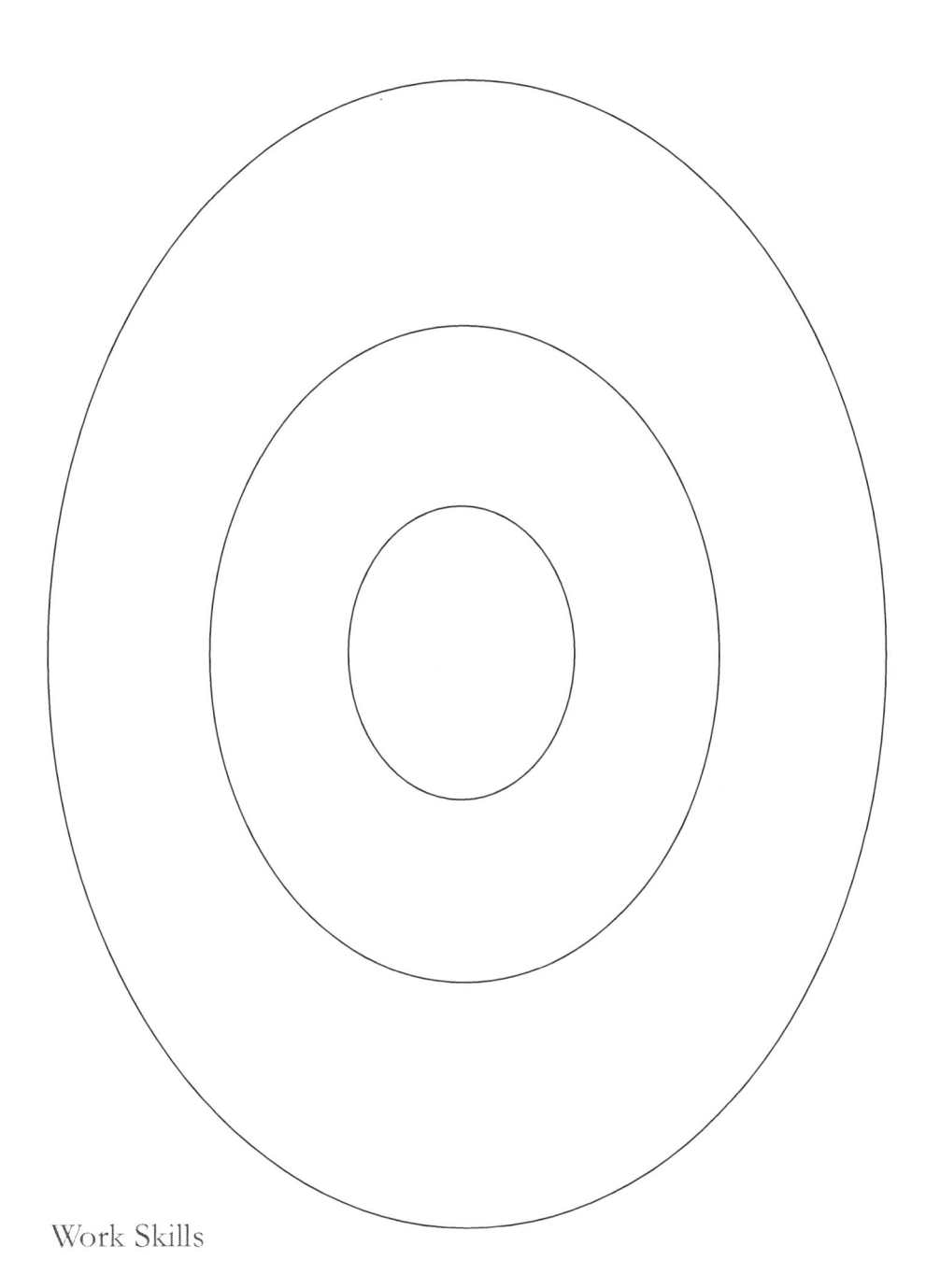

Educational Skills

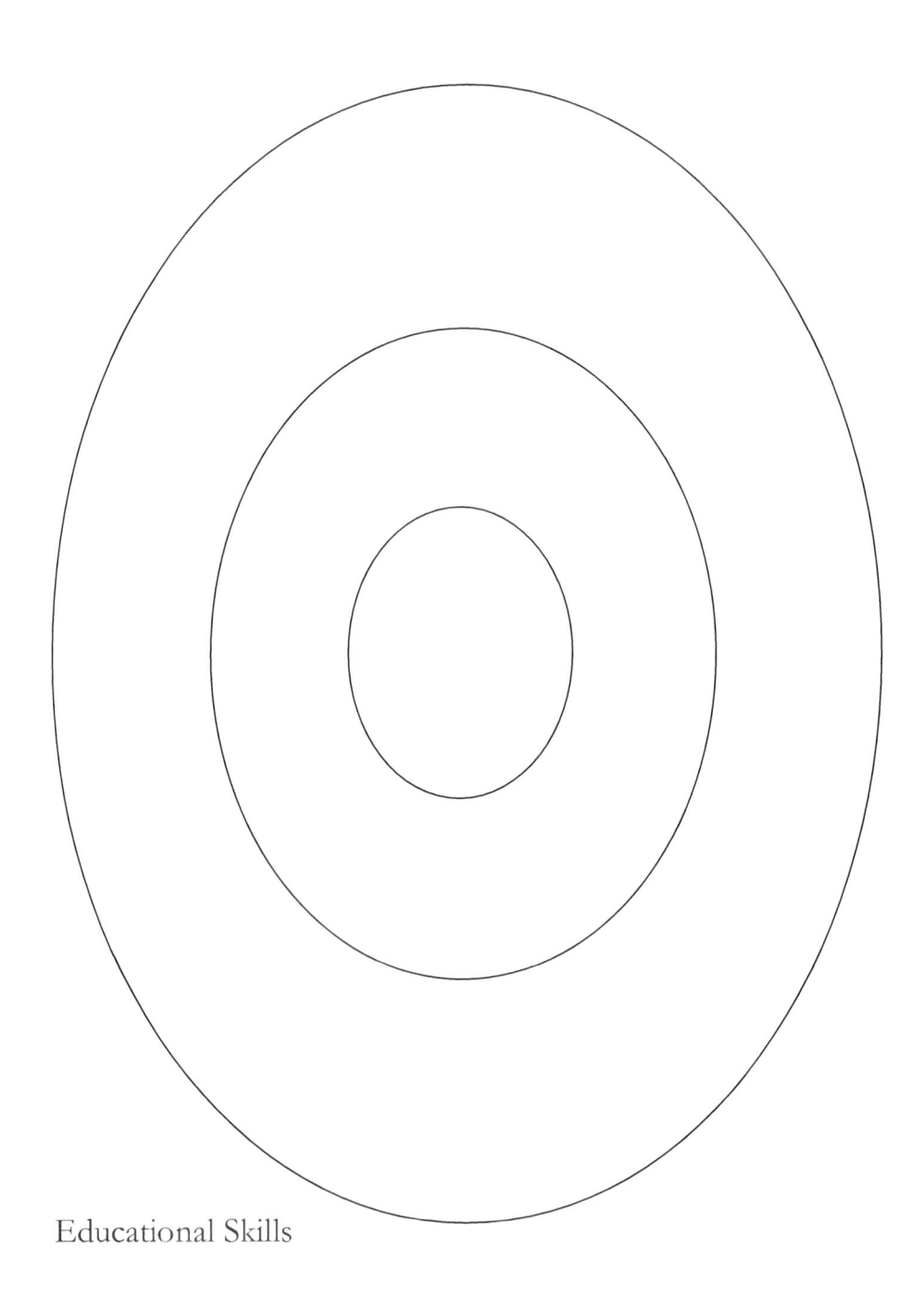

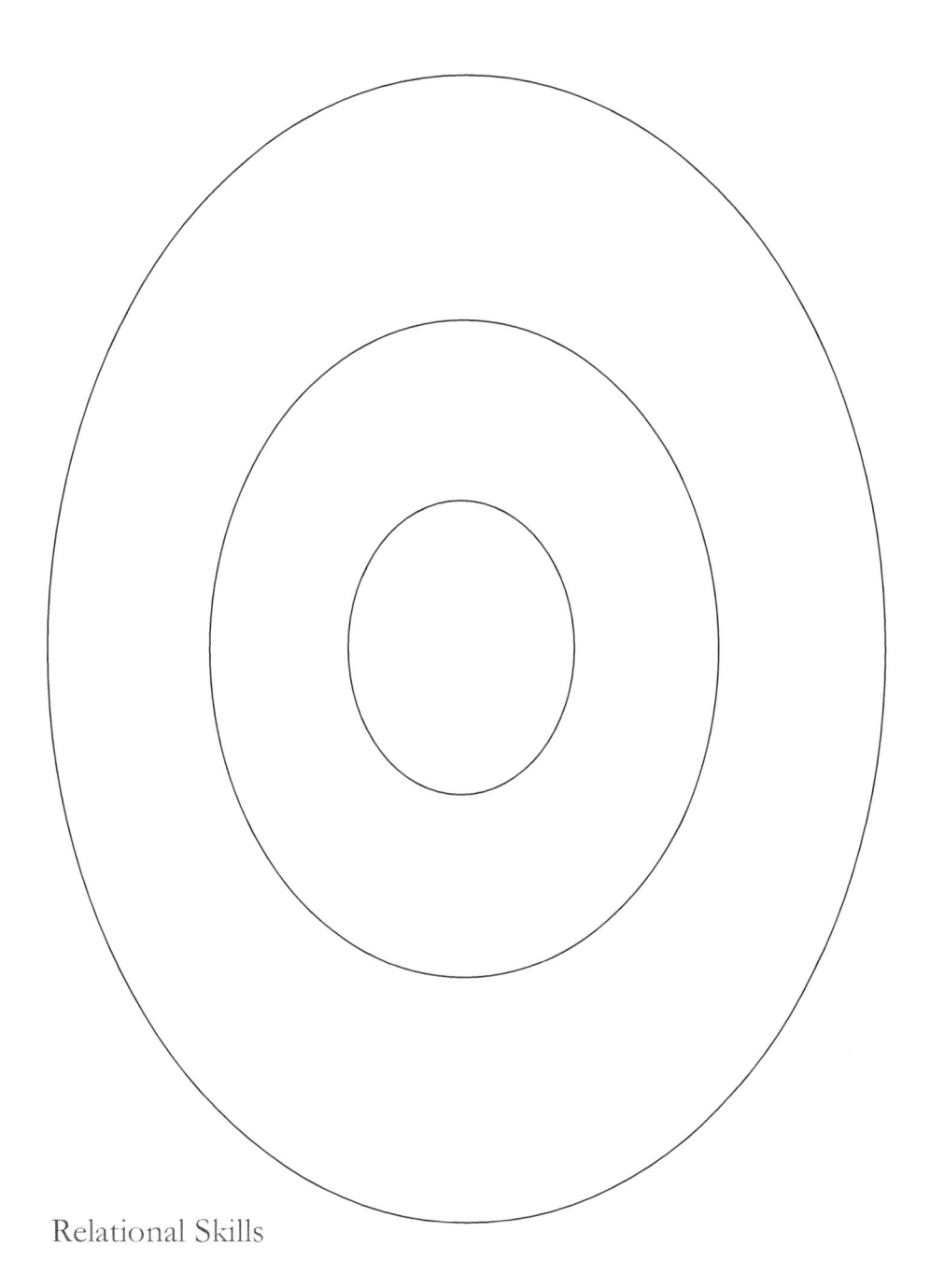

Relational Skills

Clergy Skills

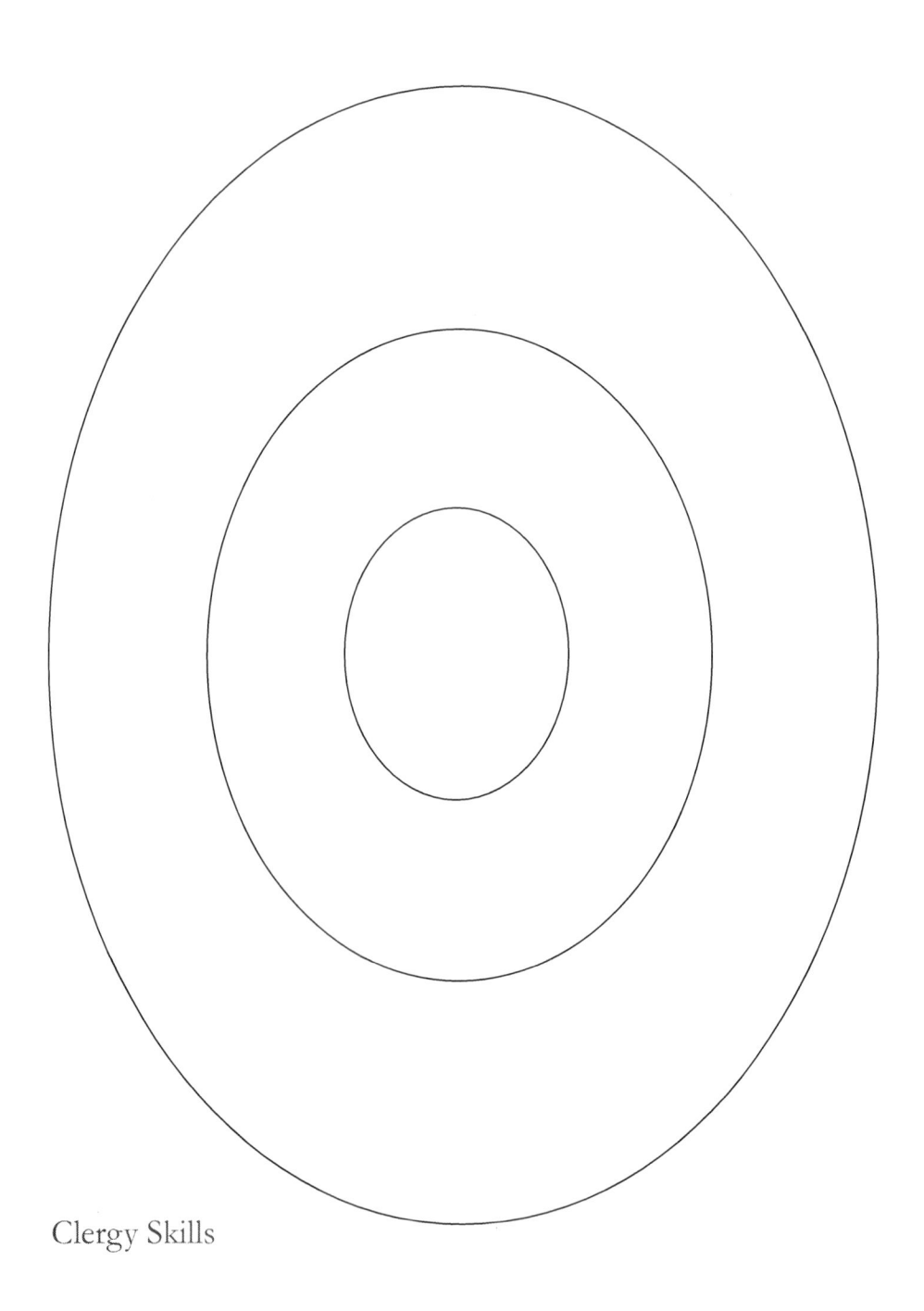

under certain situations. This raises the issue of knowing when to *refer*—that is to let your member or student know they need to talk with someone else. Clergy are often the first professional many individuals seek out for help with emotional, relational, and medical issues. Within Neopagan traditions this can be even more so as many Neopagan traditions also emphasize personal development and healing (energy work or herbal supplements for example). And this can bring about some ethical and professional challenges.

Medical Situations

Not only do most state and country laws prohibit any *medical* treatment by non-licensed professionals, but not knowing or having access to a client's complete medical history can jeopardize the individual. For example, a situation not uncommon to occur within the Neopagan environment: A few years ago, I had a student come to me complaining of widespread blood pressure problems and what should she do. I asked her about medications and any herbal supplements she was taking. Having education in pharmacology and access to pharmacological research databases, I was able to research her herbal supplements to find studies showing the herb had demonstrable impact on lowering blood pressure, sometimes unintentionally. She was able to take this information to a naturopath she was seeing, who did not know of the information, and was able to discontinue the herb and her blood pressure returned to normal. In this capacity, if you work with herbs and *prescribe* herbal (including ingesting oils) remedies to members you *must* know the research behind the herbs and assess for side-effect risks, as well as know about possible interactions between herbs and pharmaceuticals. Many herbs are metablized along the same pathways as other medications, thus increasing the risks for unsafe drug interactions, including decreasing the effectiveness of a medication. In this fashion, if you incorporate the use of herbs within your path for medicinal purposes be sure to assess your skills along the following avenue:

- Do you have sufficient training in human physiology and pathology to understand how the body processes herbs and how diseases function? Remember most physicians attend medical school for 4 years, which comprises physiology, biology, chemistry and then complete an internship and residency that generally totals another 4 years.

- Do you have access to research on herbs? There is an enormous body of research facilities worldwide where herbs are the primary focus. For example the journal *CNS Drugs* publishes a number of studies each year on the effectiveness of herbs comparable to pharmaceuticals, additionally University of Illinois maintains a database of herbs and research associated with them. Knowing the latest research and being able to access information on side effects ensures that you are keeping your members safe.

- Do you know the parameters of your state/country laws regarding diagnosis and treatment and do you qualify under these laws? If you do not qualify to legally practice you risk not only harming yourself substantially, but also harming your member. Additionally, if you do not have the legal authority to provide this treatment *and* do not disclose that to your clients then you are acting in *harm* as you are taking away *informed consent*.

Energy medicine work is another popular method of intervention associated with Neopagan traditions. It is not a licensable intervention in most states, although some states associate this type of work, such as Reiki, with massage therapy (which is often a licensable or certification-based profession). Energy medicine has a credible history of promoting healing and can be a very beneficial resource for individuals facing physical and psychological issues. To assess your limitations within this area, consider the following questions:

- Are you claiming that energy work is the *only* way for the client to recover? If so, you risk legal action if the individual does not get better and you also risk legal action for misrepresentation as a medical professional (again providing treatment claims without a license). Finally, this also risks a violation of informed consent. The individual may feel threatened if he or she seeks other methods of treatment. Research has shown that energy work is superb as an *adjunctive* treatment to other healing modalities, but little has shown that it works alone. The same can be said by allopathic medicine, which has some claim to working alone, but increasing research shows it works *better* and more *consistently* when it co-occurs with spiritual, psychological, or energetic modes of healing.

- Do you have the skills necessary for the type of energy work you are using? There is a host of reputable training institutions that provide you not only with the information on physiology and techniques, but also provide you with opportunities for supervised practical application. Whenever possible, having the opportunity to learn your skills in a supervised setting with a mentor is the ideal option as this will help you refine your abilities and increase your marketability to potential clients.

Another area of help that many Neopagan clergy provide is the use of magical interventions to assist individuals in the health challenges they face. I tend to agree with Z Budapest's perspective on this issue—she does not engage in magical interventions on behalf of her friends, students, and members as it would not be "empowering"[1]. Instead, Budapest emphasizes the importance of teaching individuals *how* to use magical interventions to effect change in their lives or working as a group to effect change, thus increasing the total available energy. If, however, you do engage in magical work it's important to consider the follow:

- Similar to energy work, are you claiming that magical interventions are the *only* way for a client to recover? Again this leads to the same issues discussed in the prior examples.

- Are you also willing to teach clients how to engage in their own magical undertakings?—if you are not, this can create an unhealthy power relationship that leads to dependency and can impact not only the quality of the magical working, but also the health and well-being of the client.

- Do you have enough experience working with magic and have you had success with it in your own life? Again, when we serve others and claim an expertise in helping and healing, those we serve deserve to know what our credentials are.

Finally, the one last area that you may encounter is when faced with members who are experiencing significant psychosocial distress. Being human carries with it the high risk for significant challenges in our family and work lives, as well as for our own mental health. Between the ages of 18 and 30, millions of individuals worldwide will develop some form of psychological illness ranging from depression, anxiety, bipolar disorder and schizophrenia. Pathological family relationships and traumatic childhoods can lead to significant problems in personality structure that become most evident during late adolescent through a person's forties. Many individuals will experience traumatic divorce, job loss, illness, and economic stress. Other challenges many individuals experience include addiction, gambling, and explosive and impulsive disorders; while families may have specific challenges associated with raising special needs children (special needs can range from mild learning disabilities to emotional and behavioral disabilities to motor and developmental challenges, such as cerebral palsy or Down's syndrome). Finally, many individuals may experience psychosocial challenges associated with gender, sexual orientation, and race. And for some, feelings of despair will become so pronounced that suicide becomes a risk. It's important first to recognize that psychological disorders are illnesses—while they are not classified as diseases yet, we do know there are demonstrable changes in the physiology of the brain—specifically in its capacity to self-regulate the amount and duration of neurotransmitters (such as serotonin, dopamine, and norepinephrine) available to make electrical connections to keep the mood and sensory system functioning at optimal level; further increasingly research is finding physical changes in brain size is present in many disorders. Finally, chronic stress can permanently alter the structure of the human immune system through over production of the stress-hormone cortisol, which can lead to a higher risk of infection to the development of cancer and autoimmune diseases. It's important that when confronted with an individual experiencing any of these high-degrees of distress and risks that you know your limits. The following list of questions can help you identify your limitations if you answer "no" to these questions or rate yourself with low comfortability:

- Do you know the warning signs of mental health crisis and how to assess for suicidality?

- Do you know how to respond when an individual claims they are suicidal or homicidal and do you feel presently comfortable handling such a situation?

- Do you know how mental health issues are treated, ranging from counseling to psychopharmacological interventions?

- Have you had counseling training, if so what type and have you had experience working within a counseling setting? Do you have a license to work as a professional counselor (social worker, mental health counselor, professional counselor, psychologist, or psychiatrist)? Most states and countries require individuals providing primary mental health treatment to have a license (similar to medical practitioners).

- Have you had experience counseling others experiencing work or family challenges—these can be formal or informal experiences—and how comfortable are you listening to others faced with marked challenges in their family or professional lives?

- How comfortable are you listening to others—are you someone who can spend long periods of time listening to others without interrupting them or turning the discussion back to your own issues?

- Do you have personal issues and prejudices associated with gender, sexual orientation, or race which could limit your capacity to help individuals?

Many challenges can be successfully helped through spiritual discussions, readings and interventions. Faith-based support for individuals and families facing profound stress is essential; however for individuals with severe problems, it typically is insufficient as the *only* method of intervention. Additionally, individuals who are actively experiencing symptoms of *psychosis* (hallucinations [hearing, feeling, seeing things that are not visible to others around them], delusions [holding beliefs about others or situations that are not true], catatonia [not moving or speaking or a reduction of motor behavior and speech], and disorganization [behavior and mood that make little coherent sense, such as dressing in the summer as if it were winter]) should be stabilized *prior* to beginning spiritual interventions and spiritual interventions should be sensitive to the individual's risk to distort reality and experience increased agitation. In most cases where mental health or social issues are profoundly distressing, referrals to qualified mental health professionals are necessary. However, this can raise an important issues for the Neopagan clergy.

If you refer patients to care whereby the therapist or psychiatrist is unfamiliar with or holds discriminatory views against the Neopagan faiths, then clients can be *harmed* in the counseling process. In this fashion, it is important for neophyte Neopagan clergy to begin networking with area mental health facilities and counselors to discuss their degree of comfort working with the Neopagan client. Additionally, Neopagan clergy should actively consider part of their service to their community as that of working with mental health facilities and counselors to provide education in the beliefs, values, and rituals of the faith to ensure that when members of their community need referrals they will be able to find professionals that not only understand their faith, but can actively support it in their clients.

Selected Online Medical Resources

National Alliance on Mental Illness (NAMI): http://www.NAMI.org
American Psychological Association: http://www.APA.org
National Institute of Mental Health: http://www.nimh.nih.gov
National Institute of Mental Health's *Medications*, an overview of psychotropics
http://www.nimh.nih.gov/health/publications/medications/medications.pdf
Basic Counseling Skills and Techniques, overview:
http://www.basic-counseling-skills.com/counseling-techniques.html
An Introduction to Crisis Counseling, overview:

http://www.crisiscounseling.org/
National Center for Complementary and Alternative Medicine: http://nccam.nih.gov/
University of Illinois's herbal supplement database, NAPRALERT http://www.napralert.org/

A Brief Word on Suicide Assessment

The following acronym can help you assess a person's risk for suicide and to communicate to emergency health officials. Remember suicide and homicide should always be reported to emergency professionals, unless you have a mental health license and can address the situation immediately through counseling. Calling your local *Emergency Screening Service* (usually the Crisis Center at your local hospital) can provide you with the professional support to make the right decision.

P—plan. Ask direct questions about the intention and plan the individual has for ending their lives. Individuals with specific plans *generally* are at higher risk for attempted and completed suicides. However, anyone who reports that they wish to harm themselves should *always* be taken seriously.

A—access. How easily does the individual have access to their proposed method for suicide? For example, an individual who owns a gun versus an individual who thinks they'll try to purchase a gun pose different risks factors. The former one is more of an immediate risk, the latter may have more time for direct interventions to help them work through their emotional distress.

M—means/methods. Different methods of harm have differing degrees of lethality. While all methods should again be taken seriously, some methods provide more time for intervention and may suggest less determination. Remember Tylenol can be fatal in a relatively small overdose and lead to permanent organ damage, additionally it is highly accessible. If an individual has stated they have already taken pills or other poisonous substances, it's important to find out what and how much was taken so that emergency personnel can make the appropriate medical intervention choices.

If you are in a situation where someone has threatened or attempted suicide, stay calm and supportive. Keep the person talking and allow them to share their challenges with you. If you are on the phone with a distress member, find out where they are, if at all possible, so that you can direct emergency personnel there. Call your local police department or signal someone around you to call so that you can stay on the phone or in the room with the person. Most individuals attempting suicide do not necessarily want to die, but feel they have no options in their lives and their current challenges or their mental illness seem unbearably painful. True empathy and compassion is absolutely critical here and to fully recognize the individual is in significant pain. It's not about convincing them to live, as it is listening to their pain and being able to "hold" it for them so that they can experience some relief. Additionally, sometimes offering to go with the individual to the hospital or to see their physician can also help encourage them to get help sooner rather than later.

Non-Medical Situations

While medical situations will often be the primary area you'll need to assess your limitations there are non-medical situations where this may emerge and a referral (discussed shortly) will be necessary. The most common one will be when you have a member of your community who either you are relationally mismatched with or the individual is struggling to connect with the community. In other words, the individual simply does not fit within the group or with you and conflicts are emerging. Hopefully, you have first exhausted all possible avenues to resolve the conflict, but sometimes personalities just to mesh. In this capacity, you do best by the individual to locate another group that might be better suited to their needs. This ensures that you are not "spiritually" abandoning them, but are caring for their well-being, as well as the well-being of yourself and your group. You are honest in acknowledging your own limitations in terms of "getting along" with everyone or "meeting" everyone's spiritual needs. We simply cannot be all things to all people and there are times when it just doesn't work. Is there any way to offset this issue before it occurs? Not really, however, you can take time to journal about "personalities" that do not mesh well with yours. We've all had experiences in our lives where we didn't get along with someone. While we may be comfortable displacing this all on the other person, relationships are always made/broken by two people. This is not to say that the two individuals share the blame equally per se, but two personalities are involved and reacting to each other. So some questions to get you journaling:

- How would your best friend describe you?

- How might a parent describe you?

- If you have a child, how might they describe you?
- If you left a relationship, how might that person describe you?
- How do you see yourself?
- Review relationships you left and describe what it was about the person that didn't mesh with you, what kind of "traits" did they exhibit?
- Review relationships that are stable in your life, what makes you and the individuals mesh or get along? What are they like?
- What are characteristics of individuals that you know you can't stand?
- What are characteristics of individuals that are difficult for you to cope with, but you can tolerate?
- To what degree do you think you can change how people are? If you think you can change people to a relatively high degree, you might find that you run into more relational challenges and mismatches.

When you review your journal, try to come up with a good description of your self and the personality of someone you might struggle with. If you operate a large group, differences between you and members may not be an issue. However, smaller groups differences can create substantial conflict. Anticipating such conflicts can go a long way to prevent them. When you know what types of personalities are irksome for you, you can assess to what degree do you need to change to work more comfortably with them. If you know you simply cannot change, then a referral at the outset of the individual requesting to join is ideal (sometimes you won't know about the full personality until later on, once conflict resolution has failed, then a referral will be necessary).

When to Refer

Referring means providing members of your religious organization with names and numbers to professionals to address the specific issues that you are either not comfortable addressing or do not have the necessary skills or licenses to address. We refer when we encounter our limitation that to attempt to "work through it" or "learn as we go" would create a potentially harmful situation for our members or limit their capacity for health and spiritual well-being. Referring means you have recognized your limitations, erred on the side of caution, and have placed your member first—it does not mean you have failed. If you find yourself encountering similar situations frequently and are having to refer many members to the same professional, it might be the universe telling you to consider exploring getting those skills to be able to provide the service yourself. You should refer with the following guidelines in your mind:

1. The individual presents with issues you are not comfortable addressing or awaken painful issues in yourself. This is very important as sometimes our members issues hit too close to home and we are still struggling with that same issue—it's very important to refer under these circumstances. I also strongly recommend you refer if you feel the individual is experiencing the *exact* same situation you've been in—this could limit your capacity to be objective and fully *hear* the individual's issues or assess their unique circumstances.

2. When the individual is exhibiting extreme emotional distress or cognitive deficits. This may be pronounced anger and an inability to deescalate, suicide ideation or plans, reckless and impulsive behavior, poverty of speech, insomnia, etc.

3. You have a fundamental dislike of some element of the individual's personality, lifestyle choices, or other characteristic of their cultural identity (race, sexual orientation, gender, age, etc.). You can't help anyone if you don't like them—pretending to like someone or being a dispassionate and distanced professional won't help.

4. When the individual's psychosocial challenges require long-term treatment. As a Clergy person your fundamental obligation is to serve the spiritual needs of *all* your members. Individuals who need long-term help should be referred to a Neopagan friendly counselor to help them work on the issues over the long-term. Pastoral counseling is generally short-term, situation based and often adjunctive to long-term psychotherapy or medical treatment.

5. When the individual has complex medical issues. If you practice healing techniques, be sure that the individual has and sees a physician to help clarify diagnoses and run the necessary tests to determine causes.

6. When the individual has a sudden medical symptom: sudden weight loss; onset of a different kind of or thunderclap headache; chest pain;

respiratory symptoms; bloody stools; spontaneous bruising; change in consciousness (alertness and orientation to time and place); uncontrollable motor movements (jerking, ticking, twitching, freezing); severe gastric pain not relieved by passing gas (or taking over-the-counter relief medications); sudden pain anywhere in the body not relieved by rest; paralysis of one side of the body; loss of speech; sudden vision or hearing changes; vertigo in an individual who has never had vertigo, etc. All of these can be indicative of an emergency medical situation.

7. When the individual has persisting medical symptoms that are not relieved by or worsened by herbal, energy, counseling, or magical interventions.

8. When the individual has a difficulty that you simply do not have the skills or legal options to address.

Remember, referring is not a failure; it's not personal either. And before concluding this section and chapter, one last note. Occasionally, you'll have a member who has been seeing you for emotional, spiritual, or physical help and they'll tell you they are leaving to pursue a different interventional method. It's important to take this in stride and let it go. You can ask the individual for their reasons, not for the sake of persuading them to stay, but so you can find an area to grow in, or simply let it go and give your blessing to the student or member to pursue their needs. It happens—we are a changeable species.

11
Resolving Ethical Dilemmas

"Am I serving the Deity(ies) in the quality of my service toward the Divine's religious adherents?" This is a primary question all individuals ordained as Neopagan priests and priestesses must continuously ask. In this question, we recognize that our religious group is not "ours" but rather belongs to the Divine Force we focus our devotion toward. We are the caretakers of this group and we should direct the same degree of care and reverence for the group as we would toward our Deity(ies). As a priest or priestess, we are gifted with the call to serve and to make more visible the presence of the Divine Force in the world around us. When we act toward our covens or groups with a consciousness that they all embody the Divine Force, we are ultimately reminding ourselves our primary role is to *enable* individuals to experience and manifest the Divine in their lives. We do not seek to *exploit* our call and perceived authority. When we consider the role of the priest and priestess as one who enables his or her members to more deeply experience the Divine, we inevitable encounter ethical challenges that require negotiating and fostering this relationship. And ethical challenges can undermine one's capacity to serve the Divine that is without and within.

Ministerial duties carry with them the expectation of greater moral standards. Research from other faiths have consistently shown that members of religious groups expect their clergy to exhibit higher standards of moral conduct both in their professional and their personal life. Indeed, research has shown that for many professional clergy moral lapses often lead to dissolution of their leadership roles and often their congregations. Part of this issue is a problem with the perception that the clergy *are* themselves reflections of the Perfection of the Divine, rather than human beings *seeking* greater wholeness and divine connectiveness themselves; as such this may be an artifact of faiths that create unrealistic and inhuman standards for their clergy rather than allow the clergy to be examples of how to connect with the Divine and manifest the divine in human ways. Clergy are imperfect, as we discussed in the previous chapter. In this fashion,

Neopagan faiths provide a potential advantage not visible in other traditions in that these faiths often centrally value and sacrelize many of the human behaviors that are seen as requiring suppression in other faiths. Nevertheless, Neopagan faiths centrally hold that while there are no restrictions on behavior *per se*, there is the requirement that any behavior engaged it must not *harm* another. As such, Neopaganism requires the capacity for continuous ethical reflection and this capacity for ethical reflection is what the priest and priestess must convey and model to his or her members. We can think of the call for ethical conduct on the part of the priest or priestess as being one of modeling ethical decision-making within the framework of the Neopagan tradition or faith one practices and teaches. This call requires each of you to consistently examine and reflect upon three critical questions::

1. What are the ethical challenges in the current situation, if any?

2. What are my options to resolve these challenges and how do I know if I am making the right decision? and

3. How can I improve upon my capacity to make the right decision?

Let's now explore the challenges raised by these questions and issues.

What is an Ethical Dilemma?

In the prior chapters, we have examined several specific issues that are typically associated with raising a red flag regarding potential areas of ethical violations and challenges. However, a simple list of right and wrong behaviors is typically insufficient in dealing with the realities of human relationships—not all situations are black and white–either/or. Becoming a Neopagan clergy person, means also becoming competent in making the best decisions for the individual one spiritually serves, for one's faith, and for oneself. Negotiating these three obligations can be tricky.

As we briefly touched on in our chapter on Multiple Relationships, there are times when maintaining a strict clergy role in the small Neopagan community one serves is nearly impossible. Additionally, there may be a time when you have a highly motivated minor interested in studying with you, but their parents are nonsupportive. This raises the tension between all three areas of responsibility. On one hand, you need to assess whether it is in the minor's best developmental and spiritual interest to learn from you; you also need to determine whether parental consent is legally and spiritual important; you will also need to assess your own competency teaching minors; and you will need to know what risks you assume should a parent not be informed and learn about the situation after the fact. When situations emerge where we cannot easily determine a right or wrong path, we are faced with what is known as an ethical dilemma.

In beginning our discussion, one way to frame ethical dilemmas is through what is known as **systems thinking**. This is an unusual approach to exploring ethical dilemmas, in that it emerges from research on computer modeling of human and organizational behavior; nevertheless it has some important and instructive properties that are beneficial for those becoming Neopagan clergy. Systems theory holds that individuals within a defined organization operate based on set behavioral and thinking processes that are created within and supported by the larger organization. The underlying parameters for these behavioral and thinking processes are known as *archetypes*. These are "simplified models of organizational processes"[1] that allow individuals within an organization to determine the best behaviors to deploy under a specific set of circumstances. Archetypes are understood temporally as defining patterns of organizationally supported behaviors that can be seen over time. In this fashion, systems theory archetypes, when applied to an organization (or by that matter *any* group of people who have specific group roles), provides a way to understand broad patterns of behavior as well as predictions about what behavior is likely to occur in a given situation. When we specifically apply this to the subject of ethical dilemmas we can think of this in three specific ways.

The first way we can apply this theory is through exploring the ethical issue as it arises within a specific organizational framework. In this fashion, when we are faced with ethical dilemmas, we can look at the specific structure of the religious group and tradition we are in care of to determine what aspects of this organization have supported the *emergence* of the ethical ambiguity and dilemma *and* what does this organizational structure, as it has been set up, say about how to address the dilemma. In this capacity, we can look at this first assessment from the perspective of examining what factors within the organizational system may be involved in shaping the dilemma or fostering it. For example, if you find that you are struggling with reporting suspected child abuse by one of your members to the authorities—you need to examine what aspects of the religious group system are inhibiting you from engaging in protective behavior (we can also apply the systems theory to increasingly larger levels of society, which in turn also help us to examine elements of our behavior that may transcend the clergy role). Another way we can ask this question is as follows: what is it about the persons involved in *this* place of time in *this* system that has/is given/giving rise to the ethical dilemma?

The second way of applying the theory is to examine our own internal issues, past experiences, and capacity to *predict* the processes of the system and how they impact the creation of ethical dilemmas. In this fashion, we need to examine what factors in us have supported the emergence of the ethical dilemma (we'll be looking more at this in the section entitled *Reflexivity*). In this fashion, this theory of ethical dilemmas reminds us that we must evaluate ourselves and what role we might play in creating, shaping, or continuing the dilemma.

The final way of applying the theory is to examine the characteristics and behaviors of the other individual(s) participating in the dilemma. If the ethical dilemma involves a specific person or group of people—we need to examine their dynamics and ways of acting, thinking, and feeling in the world to understand the factors that gave rise to the dilemma. As we would examine ourselves, we also need to consider a wide range of aspects of the other individuals involved in the situation.

Systems Theory ultimately holds that organizations function in interconnective ways of various feedback systems—whereby at each level of the organization, information and behavioral standards are being set, reinforced, and changed (see Fig. 11-1). These might be thought of as microchanges within the system. In contrast, organizations also have macrochanges—these are changes that occurs systemwide (for example a Neopagan organization may change its theological orientation). Macrochanges typically occur over long periods of time and tend to impact the entire system. Micro- and macro- changes are often present when an ethical dilemma emerges. Ethical dilemmas are often more likely to emerge during change periods of an organization.

Systems Theory also holds organizational systems fall within a continuum of openness and closedness. A closed system experiences changes due to internal structure and embedded participants; while an open system experiences change from outside its organization. Most Neopagan religious communities are closed—due to a general emphasis on silence, limited public advertising and public ritual, and keeping out of the public eye. Closed systems can be more prone to fracture and more disrupted by new members entering into the system, bringing with them "external" factors. Closed systems can run the risk of increased rationalization and ethical violations due to the lack of potential public scrutiny (for example, the Catholic Church is a closed system that fostered and permitted widespread sexual abuse, which was only addressed after the system became open); while open systems can risk an inability to make decisions due to too many opposing interests and influences.

One important systems archetype that has been argued as helping to understand ethical dilemmas is the **Drifting Goals Archetype.** Within an ethical context, this archetype indicates that the ethical principles and standards established and maintained by an organization drift over time. In other words, members of

Resolving Ethical Dilemmas 139

Ethical Dilemma/ Challenge → **Organizational Impact**

Ethical Problem Solving

Others' Impact ← **Your Impact**

Fig. 11-1

the organization begin to let the standards slide and lose their focus. As individuals lose their focus on the ethical standards, systems theorists suggest we see a rise of ethical dilemmas emerge. Organizations then lower standards, rather than correct the underling *systemic* problems. Within this frame of reference an ethical dilemma could indicate a problem in the organization that needs to be addressed; however, it is important to recognize that while a Drifting Goals Archetype is an important place to explore an ethical issue that has emerged, it may not reflect or explain ethical issues that could arise between you and a specific member.

Most ethical dilemmas emerge due to increasing complexity of the social interaction or system and often competing or incompatible issues. Ethical dilemmas often emerge at the intersection of issues associated with "human cost, risk, social justice, and limited resources"[2] where an individual must assess a multifaceted situation. For example, a mature adolescent who sincerely wants to learn your Neopagan tradition, but whose parents are nonsupportive, raises issues of religious freedom, the assessment of risk to you from parents, issues of adolescent autonomy and confidentiality, and the challenge of how to deploy your own resources to help an adolescent (see Fig. 11-2). In this capacity, ethical dilemmas are often complex and require us to assess the nuances of the situation. Neopagan clergy often face an additional challenge of being relatively isolated in obtaining feedback from other clergy members to help them process these types of situations. This places a greater pressure on the Neopagan clergy to define their ethics and maintain them and makes risks for ethical violations more likely (think again the challenge raised by a closed system).

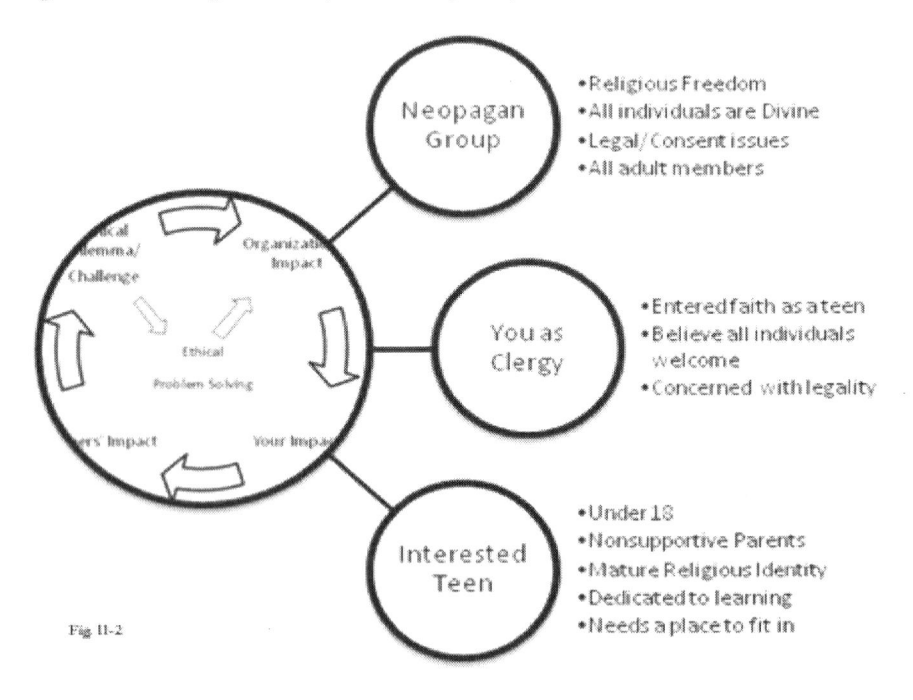

Fig 11-2

Reflexivity

Reflexivity is a term that refers to our capacity to self-reflect on characteristics of ourselves, our behaviors, thoughts, feelings, values and beliefs, and social circumstances that can and do impact our relationships with others. When we contextualize reflexivity within a systemic approach to identifying and examining ethical dilemmas, we are recognizing that what makes us different from the person(s) involved in the ethical dilemma makes a difference. When we consider the reflexive elements of an ethical dilemma, we are owning up to the elements of ourselves that have contributed to the ethical challenge, as well as attempting to ensure that our own specific needs do not undermine the needs of the situation and the individual(s) involved. One helpful strategy to encourage reflexivity within an ethical dilemma is what is known as the Ethical Genogram[3].

A genogram is a diagram of one's family-of-origin and one's current family upon which one writes down a wide range of *inherited* and *learned* values, biases, cultural experiences, significant events, etc. Additionally, in a traditional therapeutic genogram, one may utilize specific types of lines to connect oneself to others in your family to describe the type of relationship one has had with them. It is a common therapeutic technique in family counseling, as well as a primary technique for therapist training. Within an ethical genogram the focus is on what one has learned about ethics and moral action from one's family-of-origin. Specifically, within an ethical genogram, reflexivity is encouraged along the following broad ethical principles:

- Beneficence: doing what is in the best interest of your religious member or group, your faith, and other valued interests in your faith.

- Nonmalfeasance: doing no harm to your member(s) or other significant individuals/places.

- Justice: advocating for your member's rights, the rights of your religion, and the other salient rights determined by your faith beliefs.

- Autonomy: empowering members in your faith community and encouraging their capacity for self-determination.

- Fidelity: engaging with the members of your faith community and nonmembers in an authentic and truthful fashion.

I advocate expanding your family genogram to also include significant mappings of the social groups you belong to and which have shaped your self-identity and values (consider adding your work from Chapter 3). In this fashion, when you are finished drawing your genogram, you should have yourself linked to your current family, family-of-origin, and any significant social groups. Once this is done, take time to jot down next to each person and group what they have conveyed to you about ethics and ethical principles (consider both positive and negative contributions; and identify which individuals or groups have been the most important in shaping your views). This exercise can be repeated based on specific ethical dilemmas that emerge, particularly when you are having difficulty finding a clear path for yourself.

Figure 11-3 illustrates a mock-up genogram. In it you'll see key family members identified (and again you can add organizations, cousins, and a host of other relatives and individuals and invent your own ways of signifying the relationships). In the genogram, text is noted that describes key values or ethics demonstrated by members in the family. For example, the father is defined as "patriarchal" or having a "protestant work ethic". Additionally, the lines between individuals indicated close relationships or conflicted ones. The railroad tracks indicate a close emotional bond that is positive, the ragged edges and more harsh lines indicate hostile, conflicted, or abusive relationships. It's important to create some method for illustrating the relationships with your family members as relationships also communicate ethics (how we *treat* others). When I've worked with families or individuals on their own genograms, I often encourage them to be as creative as they wish and to use their creativity to help depict elements of these relationships. When you apply this to an ethical dilemma, you can also write the dilemma on the top of the page and then identify how each of your family members might respond to it. This can help you sort out unhealthy and healthy influences that might shape your specific response to the dilemma—thus warding off potential problems in its resolution.

Whether you opt for the Ethical Genogram method or not, the key is to always take time *before* you seek to resolve an ethical situation to process how you feel and what you are thinking about the situation. When we fail to do this, we often set the stage for further challenges associated with the ethical dilemma. In keeping with the idea of systems theory, our own poor responses that are impulsive or blind can impact not only the immediate situation, but also the organization as a whole—your members, your whole system. And this can set the stage for increased challenges within the system. Additionally, keep in mind that every system is linked to other systems in varying degrees of influence and potency. For example, your membership are linked to their own family systems. If they have a rotten day in ritual because an ethical dilemma got out of hand, chances are high that this will influence and negatively impact their own family system when they go home. As such, it is critical that as the leader of a Neopagan group, you always take time to reflect on your behavior, feelings, and decisions to ensure they will do the *least* amount of harm possible in a situation—and by this, impact the least number of individuals in a negative fashion, have minimal impact on any other linked system, and have a temporally finite impact (that is the impact lasts only a short duration of time).

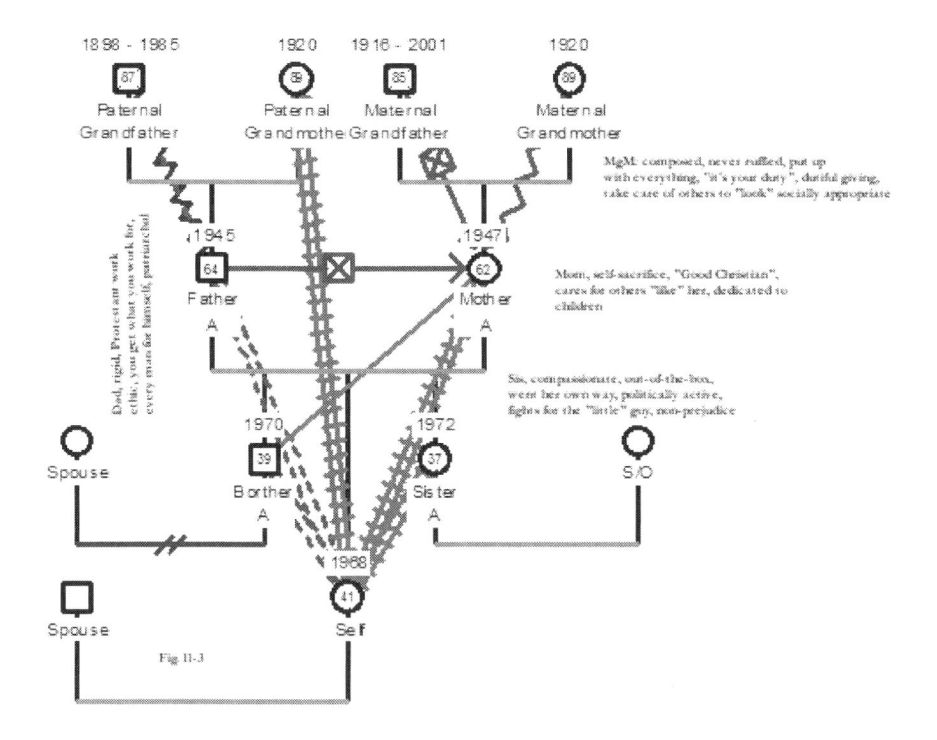

Fig. 11-3

Ethical Wholeness: Integrity

Another dimension of reflexivity is **ethical wholeness**. This is another way of describing having integrity. Integrity ultimately means the capacity to *integrate* issues of character, behavior, and theo/alogical vision into an ethical whole. Through this wholeness we are able to not only address specific ethical conflicts, but we are also able to *live* a life that is consistent with our religious beliefs and our relationship to the Divine. In this capacity, ethical wholeness means we actively look toward cultivating a personal life that is a reflection of our spiritual faith, which means we address ethical issues from the perspective of a non-conflicted or mature religious identity and faith in our beliefs; as such we literally form a *whole* sense of self—one that is secure in its religious center and one that also recognizes the responsibilities of religious leadership. Let's break this down into smaller concepts.

Ethical wholeness begins with character (see Chapter 3). Character refers to who we are and how we wish to be. When we encounter an ethically sticky situation, we must ask *how do we want to be in this situation*, before we ask *what should I do*. Character reflects the sum total of our *expressive ethics*, known commonly as virtues—personality traits that are defined as moral and guide our behavior. It's important to recognize that personality traits and character suggest an intractable element of our being; this is not entirely true. Our character/personality is continuously shaped by our actions and by the actions of others. There is a central challenge associated with character and the assumption of the clergy role. Being a Neopagan priest or priestess is *both* a social role *and* a divine calling. This can create tensions within character as it contributes to ethical wholeness. On one hand, our role is socially functional and thus it may fulfill personality needs to be liked, to have authority, and to be accepted. On the other hand, our divine calling often guides our underlying internalization of virtues and our drive to manifest this in *all* our actions. When our social role trumps our divine calling, we are more likely to engage in problematic and inconsistent ethical decision-making processes. We may be more concerned with preserving our authority over conducting ourselves in a manner that is consistent with our faith and thus would be considered ethically right. We may refrain from making difficult choices that may upset someone if we feel greater need to be liked than to manifest what is *ethically* right within our faith. Finally, there can be tensions between what is viewed as socially ethical and what is viewed as spiritually ethical—this emerges often because of differences in emotional saliency between these two areas coupled with how we think about ourselves in these situations. For example, we may feel a greater emotional need for social acceptance because we *think* of ourselves as less socially acceptable or think that others view us this way. Thus if an individual feels a marked split in character between social self and religious self, these conflicts can become highly problematic. Character is what grounds ethical decision making and aids us in committing to a decision. If we make an ethical choice that is inconsistent with our sense of *who we are* and *what we believe*, chances are high that we won't be able to follow through with the actions required.

Ethical wholeness also involves behavior. Behavior emerges directly from who we are. Who we are informs what we believe, what we see/perceive, and how we understand a situation. This will also involve how we define what is good and what is bad and, in the case of Neopaganism, what defines and delimits the concept of *harm*. For most of us, a majority of situations are processed automatically and responded to immediately—thus there may be no time between encounter with an ethical situation and our behavior. Character typically operates unconsciously. When we consider ethical dilemmas, we are often attempting to interrupt the cycle between situation and behavior to better elucidate (to reflect upon) the issues of character and thus ensure consistent and effective ethical action that also reflects a growing sense of religious identity and commitment coupled with a deeper understanding of the underlying theo/alogy of one's faith.

The final element of ethical wholeness is theo/alogical grounding. Neopaganism poses some unique challenges that are not necessarily visible in other traditions that have a centralized sacred text and beliefs. Neopaganism is a cluster of a wide diversity of smaller beliefs with some general commonalities—this puts a substantial pressure on the individual priests and priestesses to take time to define their theo/alogical core beliefs and concepts. These concepts should provide viable means of instruction on how to live a fulfilling life and how to cope with life's challenges; additionally they should be able to inform the boundaries of ethical living. And it is the underlying theo/alogical considerations that should provide a priest and priestesses guide to ethical living. Religious ethics writers consider this aspect of ethical wholeness as *moral vision*[4].

When we create ourselves into an ethically whole person, we are essentially integrating our character, our action, and our moral vision together into whole. Ethical wholeness provides us with a sense of continuity in our lives and a capacity to *demonstrate* to our students and members that our faith is livable—it is something that can guide our lives, not something we simply do intermittently or at a ritual. It is from this wholeness we are prepared to address ethical dilemmas; however, while this wholeness should help inform our possible decisions, it should not become our *sole* source of information. In other words, we cannot simply make an ethical decision based on our personal internal and lifestyle choices, we need to fully hear the scope of each unique situation. As such, we can think of ethical wholeness as what guides *our* personal behavior to ensure that we do not find ourselves at the center of hypocrisy and amoral action. Ethical wholeness refers to how we *live* our lives in an ethical fashion; while ethical decision making refers to how we apply our ethical wholeness to complex situations with others.

Activity: Applying the Ethical Wholeness Venn Diagram

Grabbing your journal again, take some time to write about the three integrated elements of ethical wholeness by copying the illustration in Figure 11-4. In each circle write down descriptive words that describe you within each sphere's heading. In the overlap areas, describe how each heading interacts with the connected other. This provides you with a basic vision of your ethical wholeness. Further on in this chapter are sample ethical dilemmas you might encounter as a Neopagan Priest/ess. Utilizing those problems, return to this diagram and journal about how those would need to be resolved to be consistent with

Fig. 11-4

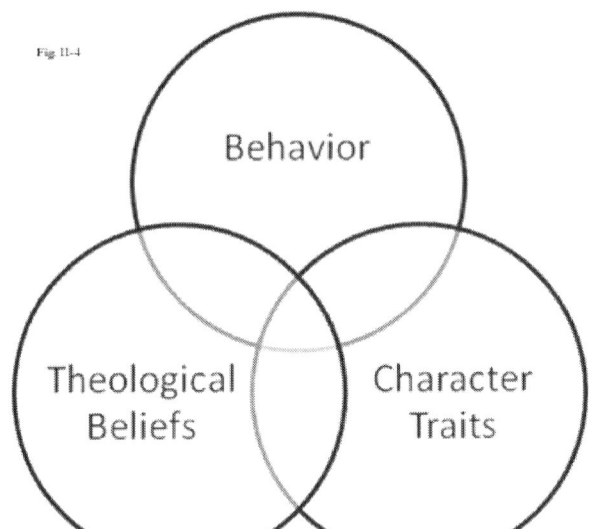

[Venn diagram: Behavior, Theological Beliefs, Character Traits]

your vision of wholeness. Consider whether this is realistic or not and how might it impact the individuals involved in beneficial or harmful ways.

Ethical Decision-Making

Ethical decision making refers to a systematic process of exploring a morally complex or ambiguous situations to determine the best course of action—in short, when we encounter a dilemma. As discussed, for most priests and priestesses, decision-making strategies become important when we are confronted with questionable or ambiguous situations with our members, when members come to us with challenging situations they need help with, or when we are faced with social situations that in general conflict with our underlying ethical wholeness. There are a substantial number of models to guide decision making; in this section we'll look at seven widely researched models.

Decision Tower[5]

This is a model (see Fig, 11-5), utilized largely within religious settings, involves exploring a situation from four levels that lead to possible resolution options. The first level refers to describing the dilemma. This asks the priest or priestess to spend time carefully examining the specific elements of the dilemma at hand. Optimally, you would take time to write a complete accounting of the situation and take time to carefully and specifically describe the situation that is causing the ethical dilemma. Once this is complete, you would move on to level two. Level two refers to values and how your personal values have shaped your understanding of the situation. During this stage, you would assess how your personal biases and your own personal goals for the situation's resolution are

Fig. 11-5

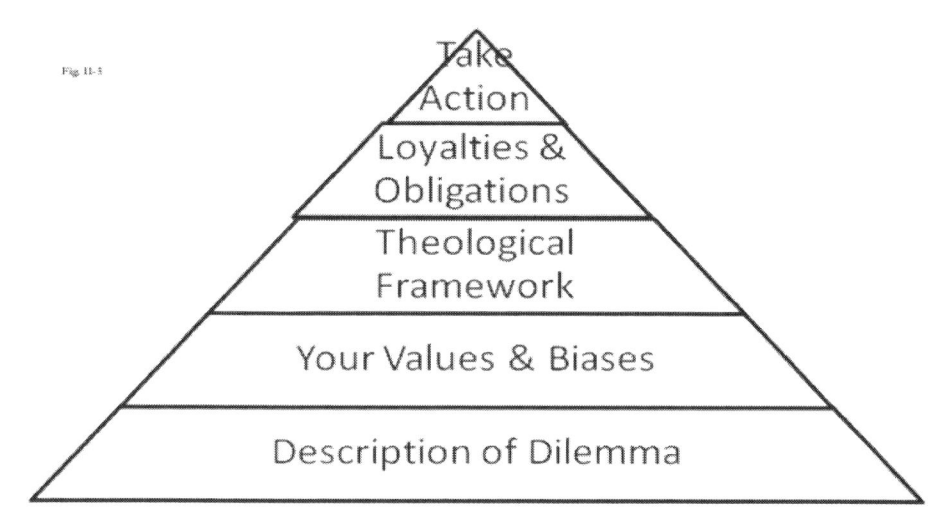

```
         Take
        Action
     Loyalties &
     Obligations
      Theological
       Framework
   Your Values & Biases
    Description of Dilemma
```

influencing how you are viewing the situation and the possible outcomes you hope to see happen. At this stage, it can be very important to obtain additional perspectives from colleagues to help further process the dilemma. Level three is the theo/alogical framework. As clergy, when you engage with individuals in this context, your religion should always be a visible aspect of your decision making. When individuals come to you for help, they are seeking spiritual interpretation, not simply mundane support. Additionally, if you are living ethically whole, your spiritual beliefs will impact how you perceive a situation and thus there should be transparency of this element in your decision making. Finally level four and perhaps the most salient of the three is termed as *loyalties*. This refers to elucidating any underlying social conflicts you may have—are you, for example, fearful of being disliked, etc. Once these four levels are assessed, you can begin to brainstorm solutions to the ethical dilemma. The challenge of this model is that there is no reflection involved on consequences. Thus it assumes the moral fortitude and rightness of the clergy without requiring the clergy to consider the actual consequences of each of these possibilities. This is critical if we are to apply this in an ethically whole fashion, which does encourage reflexivity.

Rational Model[6]

This model (see Fig. 11-6) is based on viewing all ethical dilemmas as capable of being resolved with careful pragmatic application of guidelines, rules, or ethical codes. One could call this *applied decision making*. In order to apply these

Fig 11-6

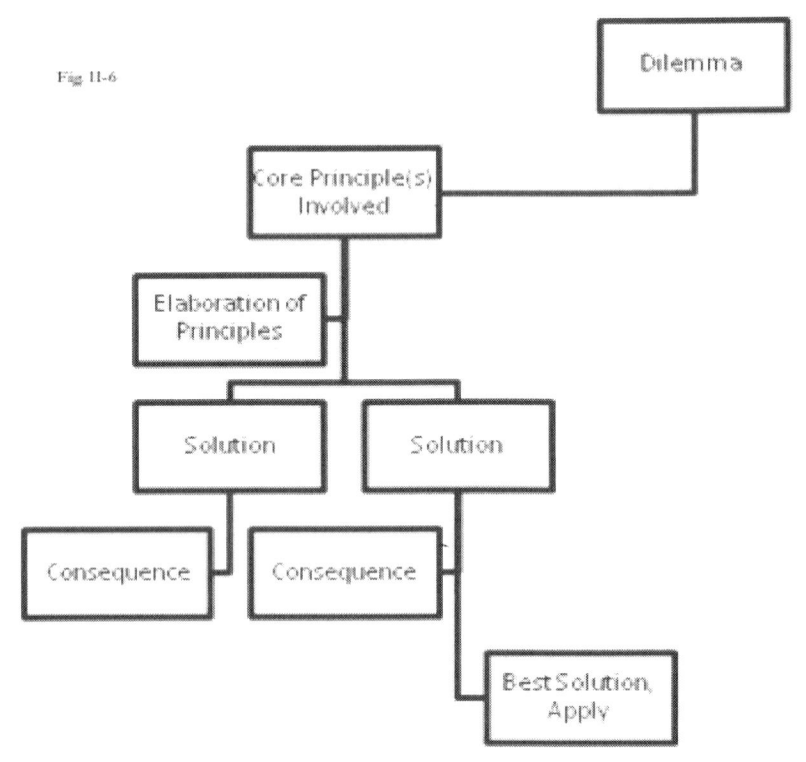

```
Dilemma
  │
Core Principle(s) Involved
  │
Elaboration of Principles
  │
  ├── Solution ── Consequence
  │
  └── Solution ── Consequence
                    │
                 Best Solution, Apply
```

guidelines, one would identify the core elements of the dilemma that reflect a principle of a guideline or code. If we were to overlay this model within a theo/alogical framework, we would consider principles as core theo/alogical frameworks and ethics. For example if applied in a religious setting, one might identify whether the dilemma reflects a problem associated with professional boundaries, competency, relationship with members, theo/alogical commitment, etc. Once these principles are identifies, one would systematically exam the delineated rules to help determine a course of action. Rational decision making involves the following steps: (a) problem identification—a description of the dilemma; (b) identification of core principles—how the problem relates to an underlying guideline, ethical code, or law; (c) elaborate the specific elements of the core principles the dilemma touches upon; (d) develop a range of possible solutions based on direct guidance from the applied codes; (e) assess the consequences of each possible solution and determine the *best* option based on this assessment; (f) re-examine this chosen course of action to reconsider all possible consequences; and (g) engage in the action. The challenge of this model for Neopagan clergy is that for most, there are no elucidated codes or guidelines and the high variability between traditions. This does not mean that a tradition cannot define a code (discussed in the final chapter), but it does mean that *before* this model can be fully implemented a guideline must be developed. This then creates a second problem in that if we rely solely on a code or guideline then we have to assume that this document is capable of addressing *all* situations. This can lead a priest or priestess to fail to carefully consider all possible elements of a situation and become overly reliant on a guideline that may in fact be imperfect.

Virtue Ethics Model

This model is similar to the ethical wholeness perspective, with the exception that such a view is applied to situations outside oneself. As such, one would approach an ethical dilemma from the view that one will act ethically if they have sufficient ethical virtues (those expressive elements of character, such as openness, honesty, trustworthiness, etc.). There are no steps; rather emphasis is placed in the assumption of the individual's good judgment and professionalism. When applied to the priest or priestess, this would mean an assumption that one's sense of duty, religious identity, and professional ideals would guide one to always make the best choice. The challenge with relying on this model is there is little reflection, little consideration of the unique aspects of a situation, and the assumption that one will always act in boundaries of their implied professional conduct. This tends to be a model that I strongly discourage individuals utilizing as it ultimately inhibits your capacity to carefully analyze and examine each situation and recognize one's personal biases and assumptions that are *always* at work in how we process the world. Further it fails to encourage examination of consequences and thus undermines our capacity to understand whether any *harm* will emerge due to our actions.

Social Constructivism Model

This model (see Fig. 11-7) holds that all decisions are influenced by social events. In this model, a priest or priestess would seek to understand what social elements gave rise to the current dilemma and what social elements might support its amelioration. This model emphasizes a bidirectional reflexivity, whereby one would look at their own actions and behaviors and how these gave rise to the dilemma, as well as the other person involved when the dilemma emerges within the context of the clergy role. Additionally this model also encourages a certain degree of examination of how one's theo/alogical concepts might increase/decrease an ethical dilemma. Typically, the resolution of a dilemma within this model requires social interventions, such as negotiating and consensus problem-solving—that is individuals work together to resolve the situation. The benefit of this type of intervention is that it allows for distributive power and responsibility; this may be ideal in Neopagan groups who are not structured in hierarchical ways. Further, this type of intervention may be beneficial when the ethical dilemma impacts a group or family system.

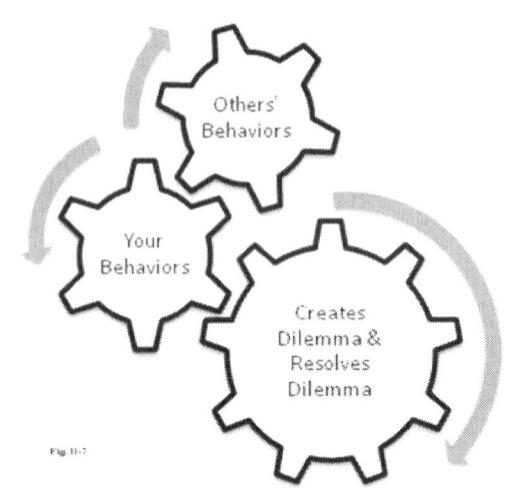

Fig. 11-7

Collaborative Model

This is a similar model to the Rational Model with the expansion that one comes to understand an ethical dilemma by engaging with a wide range of perspectives. Thus one comes to understand an ethical dilemma through multiple views of it, rather than risking encapsulation within one's own perspective and thus limiting complete understanding of the situation, one's own impact, and possible solutions. The challenge of this perspective when applied to the Neopagan clergy situation is that some situations require confidentiality and thus the priest or priestess cannot seek external help in understanding the situation. Further, while a Neopagan clergy person could discuss the situation with another clergy, most are relatively isolated and lack this collegiate support. As such, this is typically not the best model to utilize when attempting to negotiate situations that are confidential or within a hierarchically organized group. However in a non-hierarchical Neopagan community with community rules, this might be an ideal method to allow members to collaboratively resolve challenges by exploring *what solutions can we come up with together that meet the guidelines of our group?*

Integrative Model

This model unfolds in four steps: (a) defining a situation through fact finding and interpretation—this step involves both understanding one's own interpretative beliefs, while at the same time identifying the facts of a situation; (b) developing possible courses of action—this is the brainstorming aspect of resolving dilemmas and seeks to identify all possible solutions to resolving the challenge; (c) evaluating those courses of action—before implementing a course, this step allows one to uncover any competing values and blind spots that might inhibit implementing the best course of action; and finally, (d) planning and implementing the course of action. This specific model emphasizes the blending of one's personal values and beliefs with the tangible elements of a dilemma.

If we apply this to the Neopagan priest and priestess, we would examine religious elements in step one and consider the religious implications as well as their potential biasing aspects in steps three and four. In this model, the power for decision making rests solely with the clergy not with other members involved in the situation—this can lead to potentially missing other important solutions or failing to see clearly the situation from the other person's perspective. This model most closely resembles the Decision Tower, with the exception it encourages individuals to reflect on possible consequences.

Consensus Model[7]

Perhaps one of the most comprehensive models, the Consensus Model encourages a process of deeper analysis and can be applied collective or individually depending on the situation. Thus it may be ideal with some adaptations for the religious setting, whether emerging in a collective group or an individual relationship. The model relies on several key questions as follows:

- Is there an ethical dilemma? This is the primary question that begins the reflexive process of assessment.

- Who are the individuals involved in the identified ethical dilemma? Who is involved and their perspectives can profoundly impact why a dilemma emerges and also how to resolve it. For example, some personality characteristics are more likely to encourage ethical conflicts such as when an individual has difficulty with relational boundaries—they may be more prone to seeking out sexual or emotionally entangled relationships with you, placing you in a position of having to set and maintain boundaries. Taking time to assess the nature of the people involved (also consider your own reactions and feelings toward them, including any cultural elements of their person), can help clarify why a dilemma has emerged and provide key ideas for its resolution.

- What are the key beliefs, values, and other elements that the dilemma is violating or entangled with? Dilemmas emerge because there is a conflict between what is expected and required in a specific situation and what participants in the situation want, believe, etc. Be sure to consider your own beliefs and values since these are often central to the beliefs.

- What are the key aspects of the dilemma? Like all other models, it is critical to take time to clearly and completely describe the dilemma into a narrative whole that includes the participants and the elements of the dilemma. These factors should then be analyzed to help answer the following three questions:

    - Given the current dilemma, what are the possible solutions that could be utilized?

    - What are the possible conflicts, consequences, and challenges that each solution identified could raise? Be sure to examine any theo/alogical conflicts that could arise in each situation.

    - Out of all my possible options, which is the *best* option?

- From here we must evaluate our chosen option along the following lines:

    - How does my chosen option match with the underlying theo/alogical beliefs of what I practice and teach?

    - If you have an established code of ethics, How does my chosen option reflect the code of ethics and does it?

    - How is my chosen action supported by or impacted by social rules—in other words how is your choice supported or hindered by possible social effects?

    - What are my own self-interests that have influenced my chosen action and are these ethical?

If you are working collaboratively, then all of the above questions should be explored with all participants in the situation—if they all agree that the solution is viable, thus reach a *consensus* then act. If there are disagreements repeat the process of brainstorming possible solutions and evaluation. If it is solely your decision, once you have evaluated the chosen action and feel the risks or consequences are acceptable, then take action. Be prepared to re-evaluate.

Before concluding this section, it's important to recognize that any model of ethical decision making you chose, you should always recognize that for most ethical dilemmas you must make the *best* choice under a challenging situation. These choices may not resolve a dilemma in comfortable ways. As such, taking time to carefully evaluate a decision is important to better prepare you for those difficult decisions when no answer is easy. Additionally, recognize that one size doesn't fit all—flexibility is critical in decision making and not all situations are identical. Finally, there are times when time is not permitted for lengthy discussion and examination—a crisis emerges that requires immediate action. The best way to handle these situations is to always quickly prioritize risks and address the most substantial risk first (for example an individual comes to you with a clear plan for suicide) and take action. In situations where time can be taken, it's important to state the need for time to better clarify the best course of action—don't let any member press you for a rapid solution.

Case Studies

When we approach case studies (examples of possible ethical situations that can become problematic), we can analyze them through one of the above models coupled with a specific analysis of the theo/alogical implications—that is how the situation may be understood or challenges your underlying theo/alogical framework. Below, I've tried to describe some common ethical issues that could emerge within a Neopagan group setting—try your hand at applying ethical problem solving and theo/alogical examinations.

Case 1: The Case of the Differing God

John is a new member who has recently joined your tradition. John is an intense young man around the age of 25, who has just come to the Neopagan path from a rather difficult break with the Catholic Church. You admitted him to your tradition because he expressed a sincere and eager desire to learn and spoke of feeling a match between his sense of how the universe worked and the books he has read on Neopaganism. As you are the primary local group in the area, he has opted to study with you. After three weeks of attending ceremonies and being fully engaged in the ritual process, he begins to make increasingly vocal and public demands that he should be allowed to run a ritual and that he feels that the patron deities of the group should be expanded to include more Christian-based images. How do you resolve this issue?

Apply a Decision-Making Model

What are the theo/alogical Implications:

Case 2: The Case of the Lone Teen

Alice is 15 and learned about your group from a local New Age shop where you've posted a flyer. She is a relatively isolated teenager and feels that few people understand her. Her father left home when she was around five and her mother has a habit of drinking heavily. Alice feels drawn to Neopaganism and would like to study with you. How do you resolve this issue?

Apply a Decision-Making Model:

What are the theo/alogical Implications:

Case 3: The Mom

Sherri has been an active member of your group since its inception three years ago. She is an elder and carries a great deal of weight for the group. Your group has been structured as adults-only and most of the group meetings have involved adult-themed discussions and rituals and has come to fulfill an important role for members to help them cope with the stressors and challenges of being an adult. Sherri has arrived to the group meeting bringing her eight-year-old daughter and has not informed you or any other member in the group. Members are surprised and uncomfortable about the child being at the group, but feel nervous about confronting Sherri, whom they have all relied upon throughout their own training. How do you resolve this issue?

Apply a Decision-Making Model:

What are the theo/alogical Implications:

Case 4: Mutual Attraction

Michael/Michelle is a dynamic and attractive new member. He/She brings substantial experience and new ideas to the group to which the members readily respond to. He/She is a likeable and sincere person and you feel a genuine connection to the person. Over time, this connection begins to feel more like attraction and Michael/Michelle has likewise expressed they are interested in you. Taking into consideration both your current relational status *and* your role as priest/priestess in your group, how do you respond to this situation?

Apply a Decision-Making Model:

What are the theo/alogical Implications:

Case 5: A Request for Healing

Elizabeth has been a member of your group for many years and has been recently diagnosed with pancreatic cancer. She has decided that the only source of healing is through spiritual devotion and seeks your help to heal her. Her husband, however, would like her to follow-up with the cancer specialist to try chemotherapy and radiation. Elizabeth is adamant that such health interventions are simply a product of the medical machine that seeks to control individuals' lives and that she can experience a full recovery through prayer and ritual. How do you respond to this situation?

Apply a Decision-Making Model:

What are the theo/alogical Implications:

Case 6: Marriage

Jeff and Christopher have been deeply involved in the Neopagan community and in your tradition specifically. After years of being in a committed relationship to each other, they have decided they would like to marry. They come to you to officiate their wedding. Your local ordinances prohibit gay couples from marrying, how do you resolve this situation?

Apply a Decision-Making Model:

What are the theo/alogical Implications:

Case 7: The Case of Child Abuse

Bethany has been a longtime member of your group and had been active and committed to your tradition. Lately she has appeared more stressed and haggard. You ask her about what is going on and she discloses financial problems in her family and difficulty meeting her monthly commitments due to a recent change in job status. You ask about how her family is coping and she notes she is increasingly angry with her five-year-old special needs son. When asked in what way does she express this anger, she describes losing her temper and frequently hitting him. She expresses remorse and guilt over these actions, but feels unable to control her behavior and no longer knows how to respond to his own behavioral issues. How do you respond to this situation?

Apply a Decision-Making Model:

What are the theo/alogical Implications:

12
Establishing an Ethical Code

An ethical code is a set of written rules that are specific to a profession's skills, values, and definitions of what constitutes *right* behavior (normative ethics). Ethical codes can be problematic in a number of ways associated with the following factors: (a) *who* has the authority to write them; (b) *who* has the authority to assert them; (c) *how* will the code be utilized and interpreted by professionals in the associated field; and (d) *how* often will the code be revised and updated. When we consider who determines what should be in a code, we are ultimately relying on the judgment of one or several individuals to determine ethical action. This typically assumes these individuals have ethical wholeness and will develop a code without personal bias. Typically organizations guard against bias by establishing a committee of individuals to *co-create* the code—thus through the incorporation of many individuals, the code takes on a diverse perspective. However, there is typically no measurement to determine how ethically whole those are who create the code in the first place. In this capacity, codes should always be examined for underlying biases and unstated value statements through the language utilized. Further, codes should always be examined by who is left out of the group creating the code. Many brainstorming groups are homogenous in nature where members do not differ in any substantial way from each other. Members are often selected based on organizational politics, rather than skill, and many times lack substantial diversity of experience and opinion—all of which can lead to a nonviable ethical code as it no longer can anticipate a range of experiences and needs of a culturally diverse population (and when we apply this to religious codes, this could lead to narrow theological interpretations that may not reflect the membership accurately).

Second a code becomes of little use if there is no process for implementation and enforcement. Ethical codes are considered the laws or governing rules of a specific professional body or organization of members. For example, the American Psychiatric Association, the American Psychological Association, and the

Bar Association are all professional associations with enforceable codes of conduct (ethics codes). They have the capacity to sanction members, dismiss/disbar members, and in some cases revoke licenses. Each of these organizations establish a board associated with enforcing ethics violation charges brought against a member by another member or a member of the public. The degree to which an ethics code has authority to guide behavior depends upon the ability of the organization to ultimately police itself.

The third element is the actual use of the code. Ethics codes are meant to provide guidance (see the Rational Model in the previous chapter), not meant to be absolute. This provides a challenge both in the enforcement and in the use of the codes. When ethics codes are implemented literally all the time, they tend to legalize behavior and ultimately undermine the capacity of the individual to correctly interpret the situation and respond to unique factors of the situation. This leads to the application of the ethics code as a one-size-fits-all approach, which may limit its applicability in many situations. As such, most ethics codes are divided into guiding principles and specific laws. The purpose of this is that individuals must meet the standards of the guiding principles, while they may have more room to interpret and expand the specific standards of law or to develop their own sense of right and wrong to meet a situation that falls outside of these specific laws (more on this in a moment). In short, a good ethics code allows for both literal and flexible interpretations to meet the changing needs of all interactions.

Finally an ethics code that is never revised is a problematic code. Society changes as do the problems that impact a wide range of people. Ethics codes are designed to address the *most likely* situations the professional will encounter in a specific given time—the time the code is written. Over the years, the problems most commonly experienced may change or expand. A code must have some element of review and reevaluation to ensure it reflects the changing needs of the professionals and the consumers who seek out these services.

Crafting a Code

So what is in a code? Ethics codes are structured in three broad parts: **the preamble, the principles,** and **the rules.** The preamble is typically a paragraph that reflects an oath or a pledge of commitment to the principles and rules to come. When we consider this within a religious perspective, it typically restates one's connection to the Divine and how this connection informs and guides the remainder of the code. For example:

Having accepted the call of the Lord and Lady and recognizing my service to Them and the immanent manifestation of Them in my congregation and my own life, I voluntarily agree to adopt and commit myself to the following principles and actions.

After the preamble there are typically the main ethical principles your tradition upholds and a brief description and pledge to these principles. These are the primary guiding principles utilized to assess ethical dilemmas and solutions. The most common principles are:

- Fidelity: commitment to yourself, your Deity(s) and your members;

- Gratitude: your manifestation of gratefulness in your life often associated with not taking people or events for granted and for expressing a healthy sense of pride and humbleness;

- Justice: being an advocate for and an example of equality and fairness;

- Beneficence: service to and doing good for others; and

- Nonmalficence: minimizing harm.

Within Neopagan traditions there are other principles that may be added, such as:

- Mindfulness: referring to the emphasis on time orientation of valuing the present-moment and focusing on the here-and-now;

- Ecocentrism: referring to a consciousness of wholeness, interconnectivity, and earth-mindedness;

- Honor: referring to honoring the deity within and without all living things; and

- Autonomy: valuing and supporting the rights of others to choose their own course.

Principles are derived from the theo/alogical values of your tradition—what your tradition defines as core needs and requirements for *all* people. These are the primary principles that you as a priest or priestess must uphold.

The final element of an ethics code revolves around the specific rules and parameters that define your professional role. These are often broken down into four areas each labeled with their own header: (a) professional role, duties, and competency; (b) relational parameters between self and religious member; (c) relational parameters between self and colleague; and (d) relational parameters between self and community. Professional role includes a detailed list of all the requirements of a priest or priestess within the tradition you teach. In other words, in order for someone to successfully maintain this role, they must act in a certain way. This should also include requirements for continuing education and professional development. For example:

    1.1. I/He/She will uphold the principle ethics of me/him/her tradition.

    1.2. I/He/She will actively cultivate my own devotion through daily prayer, personal rituals, and meditation.

    1.3. I/He/She will honor the Divine that is immanent within me, as I/He/She honor the Divine that surrounds me/him/her through engaging in ...

    1.4. I/He/She will continue to read and seek ongoing training to refine my/his/hers skills and knowledge...

In section two, relational parameters between self and member, you might write:

    2.1. I will engage with my members in a supportive, encouraging and respectful fashion

    2.2. I will not engage in multiple relationships, unless this is in the best interest of the group or the individual.

In the third section, you would describe the parameters of your relationship to other professionals in your tradition if you have them presently. While the final section should have a few statements in how you would conduct yourself in your *professional* capacity within the community. There is substantial flexibility in how you could write your code—unlike other professional organizations, the religious community typically has a high degree of variability and many of their statements may be more abstract and written in paragraph form and in the format of a declaration of a commitment or a promise. The main challenge to consider when you are or should you write an ethics code is how well does it provide practical guidance for other professionals in your tradition. A true ethics code should be specific in terms of writing what is absolutely essential behavior and what behaviors are 100% prohibited. For example, an ethics code should have in its relationship section:

- I will not engage in sexually harassing behavior toward any member of my community that includes unwelcome and inappropriate touching, patting, or explicit comments, and other behaviors that could be mis-

- I will not engage in any coerced sexual intercourse with any member and will not use my position of authority to develop such relationships.

- I will report all cases of suspected child abuse as required by law.

- I will maintain confidentiality where not restricted by law.

It is important to recognize that whether you violate an ethical code does not depend on whether you *perceive* you have violated it or not, but whether those enforcing it and whether the impacted individual has perceived it as such.

A few final notes on the ethical code:

- Remember it has three parts—the first declares your commitment, the second declares the guiding principles of your faith that determine what is ethical; and the third illustrates specific parameters of behavior that *everyone in leadership must adhere to*.

- It should be revised and re-evaluated to ensure it remains relevant.

- It should be utilized and enforced—there's no point in having one if no one uses it to evaluate actions. Thus it often becomes important when the organization has expanded. In a small tradition or coven, a modified ethics code that reflects your commitment to your members can be dispersed to members and thus they become the enforcers for your own behavior while at the same time informing them what you will and will not do.

Create Your Own

Write your Preamble:

_____

_____

_____

Define your Principles (try to define at least 3 that are theologically grounded)

(1) _____

_____

_____

_____

(2) _____

_____

_____

_____

(3) _____

_____

_____

_____

Define the sections of your Laws—what broad categories will your laws be broken down into?

_____

_____

_____

_____

Define your laws, write at least 3 behavioral guidelines for each category you come up with:

Section One:

(1.1) _____

_____

(1.2) _____

_____

(1.3) _____

_____

_____

_____

Section Two:

(2.1) _____

_____

(2.2) _____

_____

(2.3) _____

_____

_____

_____

Section Three:

(3.1) _____

_____

(3.2) _____

_____

(3.3) _____

_____

_____

_____

Evaluate your code....

> How practical is it? Can you think of any situations where the code won't help? If so, what might help to make it more useful?

> How enforceable is it? Who will enforce the code?

What are the assumed values of the code? What does it say about your worldview? Does it have any hidden biases? Is one group of individuals favored over another in the code?

How frequently do you think your code would need updating and re-evaluation?

❧

With the crafting of an ethics code, we reach the end of this small book on introducing ethics and professional practice. A code is the bridge between the two subjects. It unifies the underlying principles and ethical spirit of your faith with the specific parameters of your ministerial role. These are inseparable aspects: ethics and practice, with the latter most closely reflecting the applied element of our ethics. To be a priest or priestess is to apply our ethical frameworks into our day-to-day lives. We live in these roles, they are not merely functional career choices—they reflect a spiritual calling and fundamental statements about how our paths interpret, intuit, and reveal the underlying processes of the universe. They enable us to model to our students and congregates not simply functional or intellectual elements of our traditions, but how our faith reflects an ever-present energy. To practice as a priest or priestess is to continuously reveal the divine through our ethical choices.

Notes

Chapter 1

1 *arête* roughly translates to reflect the ideal of goodness or virture.
2 Sayre-McCord, G. (2007). Metaethics. Retrieved from
http://plato.stanford.edu/entries/metaethics/
3 Here we must be careful when evaluating religions to recognize that some religions take strong situational, socially constructed views of morality, changing through time and thus not reflecting the central nature of the Divine, which is to be a moral constant.

Chapter 2

1 Gula, R. M. (1996) *Ethics in pastoral ministry*. New York: Paulist Press. p. 9
2 Quinn, P. (n.d.). Theological ethics, 1702–1706. Retrieved from:
http://www.routledge-ny.com/ref/ethics/entries/theologicalethics.pdf. p. 1702
3 One of the central differences *between* religions, however, is the nature of the human body. We'll see in Neopagan traditions, such as Wicca and Goddess paths, that the human body and the earthly life are equally divine and that there is no need to *transcend* these areas; rather we can awaken our conscious awareness of the Divine through increasing awareness of our world around us and our actions within the world. In this capacity, Neopagan traditions do not hold the notion that humans are dislocated from the Divine by being on Earth.
4 Orr, E.R. (2008). *Living with honour: A Pagan ethics*. Hants, UK: John Hunt Publishing Ltd. p. 63

5 We can additionally interpret chastity as the choice to *not* engage in a path—to reject something, to turn against an option, to choose *not* to experience something, to constrain oneself, to remain unclouded, for example.

Chapter 3

1 Sue, D.W., & Sue, D. (2003). *Counseling the culturally diverse: Theory and practice.* New York: John Wiley & Sons, Inc. p. 266
2 Rabinovitch, S. T., & Macdonald, M. (2004). *An ye harm non: Magical morality, and modern ethics.* New York: Citadel Press. p. 17
3 Retrieved from www.dictionary.com
4 Kluckhohn, F. R., & Strodtbeck, F. L. (1961). *Variations in value orientations.* Evanston, IL: Row, Patterson, & Co.
5 Carter, R. T. (2000). Perspectives on addressing cultural issues in organizations. In R. T. Evans (Ed.), *Addressing Cultural Issues in Organizations: Beyond the Corporate Context* (pp. 3–18). Thousand Oaks, CA: Sage Publications.
6 This varies, some Neopagan traditions hold all humans are essentially good; while others suggest we are the potential for both good and bad depending on our actions.
7 This is actually my own addition to the model based on years of clinical work with individuals of multiethnic cultural identities and as a Neopagan-based minister.
8 Again this is my own addition to the model.
9 Gula, R. M. (1996) *Ethics in pastoral ministry.* New York: Paulist Press. p. 31
10 The ATS is a Judeo-Christian–based accreditation committee, they do not oversee any other faith; however their research is of value in terms of the ministerial duties which are shared among *all* faiths.
11 1973, 1987

Chapter 4

1 Harrow, J. (2002). Spiritual mentoring: A pagan guide. Ontario, Canada: ECW Press. This is an excellent text exploring the pastoral and mentoring relationship in Neopaganism.
2 This is US law only. Individuals outside the US are encouraged to speak with their government to learn the laws for religious recognition.

Chapter 5

1 Peek, L. (2005). Becoming Muslim: The development of a religious identity. *Sociology of Religion, 66,* 215–242.
2 Not all individuals move through these stages, some may remain in the ascribed stage because those who ascribe their faith remain more important (more salient) to that individual's sense of self than a reflected-upon religious identity.
3 Rambo, L. R. (1993). *Understanding religious conversion.* New Haven, CT: Yale University Press; see also Kahn, P. J. & Greene, A. L. (2004). "Seeing conversion whole": Testing a model of religious conversion. *Pastoral Psychology, 52,* 233–258.
4 I prefer to use the term *Transition* as it is a less-loaded term associated with stereotypes about individuals who "convert" to religions being more fundamental. While this has some bearing in research associated with Christianity and Islam, it is not as visible in Neopagan traditions that tend to take a less firm group identity that must be impermeable to all other religions and hold essential "truth" claims about the nature of the Divine.
5 A large group of Hindu's that were and still are seen as outcasts of society.
6 see Kahn & Green, p. 236
7 Fowler, J. (1981). *Stages of faith.* San Francisco: Harper and Row. See also Parker, S. (2006). Measuring faith development. *Journal of Psychology and Theology, 34,* 337–348.
8 To learn more about Jean Piaget, please see *The Psychology of the Child* by Piaget and Inhelder; to learn more about Kohlberg's stages of moral development, see http://faculty.plts.edu/gpence/html/kohlberg.htm; for Erikson, *Identity and the Life Cycle* by Erikson.
9 To legally perform psychotherapy you must have at minimum a Master's degree from an accredited institution in Counseling or Social Work. To label yourself as a psychologist you must hold a PhD/PsyD from an accredited institution. For either Masters or Doctoral level counselors, you must have a license to practice psychotherapy within any state in the United States. If you advertise or practice psychotherapy outside the scope of religious parameters, you will be held criminally liable.
10 For further information on this see the work of humanistic psychologist Carl Rogers.
11 This is not the capacity to *feel* other's emotions—a common misunderstanding. Sympathy is the act of *feeling* what others feel and experience.

Chapter 6

Foucault, M. (1997). The work of representation. In S. Hall's (Ed.), *Representation: Cultural Representations and Signifying Processes*. London: Sage Publications.
2 Kanter, R. M. (1977). *Men and women of the Corporation*. New York: BasicBooks. p. 116
3 "one" being referred to an individual or to a larger group goal.
4 Warren, K. J. (2000). *Ecofeminist philosophy: A western perspective on what it is and why it matters*. New York: Rowman & Littlefield Publishers, Inc.
5 A hierarchical structure whereby an individual or group takes or assumes power over another group.
6 It is no coincidence the Wiccan tradition Starhawk co-founded is known as Reclaiming.
7 Quinn, L. (2008). 13 reasons why Pagans should vote. *The Beltane Papers, 43,* 4. Available at:
http://theBeltanePapers.net
8 Standing against does not necessarily mean protesting—it can be the simple act of practicing one's faith openly, or writing a letter to the editor about religious discrimination, or educating oneself about diverse faiths and engaging in scholarly dialogue with other religious leaders to demonstrate the religious validity of Neopaganism, or being involved in social justice movements such as environmentalism, equal rights, or world hunger to show the moral values of Neopaganism and how they can be deployed in the wider social framework. It can also be conducting rituals to end these types of social challenges or promote empowerment of an adherent who is discriminated against or setting up a Neopagan charitable organization.
9 Closed means members can only enter this class of individuals *after* achieving a certain religious degree and often passing a personal assessment by the highest-ranking member of the tradition.

Chapter 7

1 Sonne, J. L. (2005). Nonsexual multiple relationships: A practical decision-making model for clinicians. Retrieved from http://www.kspope.com
2 Clearly as a religious organization, by its nature it will discriminate along religious lines. However, many Neopagans uphold multiple religious identities and may feel fearful of exploring aspects of their identity if they feel them must choose or silence a salient part.

3 Younggren, J. N., & Gottlieb, M. C. (2004). Managing risk when contemplating multiple relationships. *Professional Psychology: Research and Practice, 35,* 255–260. pp 256–257.

Chapter 8

1 Reed, E. C. (2000). *The heart of Wicca: Wise words from a crone on the path.* York Beach, ME: Samuel Weiser, Inc. p. 42

Chapter 9

1 A ceremonial form of whipping that indicates one's willingness to submit and suffer for spiritual growth—typically utilized in very formal and high ceremonial Neopagan traditions, but rarely in most contemporary paths. I personally object to this type of action as it fosters unhealthy submissiveness, increases the risk of religious indoctrination and abuse, and is theologically inconsistent with the view of immanence—the God/dess Within.

Chapter 10

1 Budapest, Z. (2003). *The Holy Book of Women's Mysteries.* San Francisco, CA: Red Wheel/Weiser Inc. p. 7

Chapter 11

1 Bordoel, E. A., & Haslett, T. (2006). Exploring ethical dilemmas using the "drifting goals" archetype. *Journal of Management Education, 30,* 134–148. p. 136
2 Smith, J. A., Smith, A. H. (2001). Dual relationships and professional integrity: An ethical dilemma case of a family counselor as clergy. *The Family Journal: Counseling and Therapy for Couples and Families, 9,* 438–443. p. 438
3 To view examples of how a genogram chart looks and the symbols utilized, see
 http://www.genopro.com/genogram/examples/

4 Trull, J. E., & Cater, J. E. (2004). *Ministerial ethics* (2nd Ed.). Grand Rapids, MI: Baker Academic. This is an excellent book exploring ethics and the ministry—while specific to Christian ethics, it can provide some ideas for the Neopagan priest and priestess looking for ideas on establishing an ethical framework for their own specific tradition.

5 See Milco, M. R. (1997). *Ethical dilemmas in church leadership.* Grand Rapids, MI: Kregel Publications.

6 The models from Rational to Integrative are adapted from Garcia, J. G., Cartwright, B., Winston, S. M., & Borzuchowska, B. (2003). A transcultural integrative model for ethical decision making in counseling. *Journal of Counseling & Development, 81,* 268–277.

7 Chabon, S. S., & Morris, J. F. (2004) A consensus model for making ethical decisions in a less-than-ideal world. *The ASHA Leader, February,* 18–19.

About the Author

Dr. Katherine MacDowell has had a rich and varied professional and educational background. She holds both an undergraduate degree in English Literature and a masters in Counseling Psychology from Rutgers University, where she was considered an "exceptional" student with "refreshing depth". Her masters degree involves specializations in infant and child development and multicultural counseling. In addition to her masters in psychology, Kate also holds two masters of divinity and two doctorates in theology with an emphasis on Comparative Religion, Neopagan Systems, and Christian theology. She has extensively studied Feminist Theology and spent two years immersed at the Women's Spirituality Forum under the direction of Z. Budapest. Her primary theological and research focus is on the philosophical system of Religious Naturalism, as well as the impact of globalization upon theo/alogical systems. She is an ordained interfaith minister and shamanic teacher.

At this time, she is a doctoral candidate in Health Psychology. Her doctoral research has focused toward how psychology can be a viable avenue for social change and a rigorous examination of the paradigmatic assumptions of psychology that excludes Nature and the human dislocation from the Natural world. She is a member of the Golden Key National Honor Society, the Psi Chi Honor Society for Psychology, Association of Conservation Psychology, the Society for the Psychological Study of Social Issues, the American Psychological Association, the Association for the Study of Literature and the Environment, and is certified in human research by UCLA.

Outside of her own learning, she has spent more than 8 years as a professional psychotherapist and addictions counselor and has lectured widely as a professional development provider for the New Jersey Department of Education. She is an award-winning produced playwright and a produced singer-songwriter and orchestral composer. She is the author of *Witness*, a poetry collection published in August 2009.

In 2005, she was diagnosed with a progressive autoimmune disease forcing her to retire early from her clinical work. Becoming a "disabled" woman provided her with personal experience of the barriers to quality education faced by individuals with disabilities and individuals from non-middle class backgrounds. To ameliorate this imbalance, she founded Ocean Seminary College to encourage global, multifaith seminary education that is barrier free (tuition-free, online with a mixture of self-study and group courses).

To learn more about Dr. MacDowell, www.KateEMacDowell.com. To learn more about Ocean Seminary College and its mission:

www.OceanSeminaryCollege.org

Made in the USA
Middletown, DE
16 February 2016